KEEP

THE

FAITH,

CHANGE

THE

CHURCH

THE BATTLE BY CATHOLICS FOR THE SOUL
OF THEIR CHURCH

KEEP
THE
FAITH,
CHANGE
THE
CHURCH

JAMES E. MULLER
Founding President of VOICE OF THE FAITHFUL

and

CHARLES KENNEY

RODALE

Printed in the United States of America
Rodale Inc. makes every effort to use acid-free ∞, recycled paper ♻.

Book design by DesignWorks

Library of Congress Cataloging-in-Publication Data

Muller, James E., date.
Keep the faith, change the church : the battle by Catholics for the soul of their church / James E. Muller and Charles Kenney.
    p.   cm.
  ISBN 1–57954–890–3 hardcover
  1. Voice of the Faithful (Organization)   I. Kenney, Charles.
II. Title.
BX809.V65M85   2004
282'.09'0511—dc22   2003025687

Distributed to the book trade by St. Martin's Press
2   4   6   8   10   9   7   5   3   1   hardcover

Visit us on the Web at www.rodalestore.com, or call us toll-free at (800) 848-4735.

WE **INSPIRE** AND **ENABLE** PEOPLE TO IMPROVE
THEIR LIVES AND THE WORLD AROUND THEM

We dedicate this book to the original founders of Voice of the Faithful—a devoted group of Catholics who, in their anguish over the revelation of deep flaws in their beloved church, sought help from one another and the Holy Spirit, and brought forth an organization that offers hope for a better church.

Kathy Aldridge

Paul Baier

John Berry

Bill Cadigan

Ann Carroll

David Castaldi

Tanya Chermak

Peggy Connolly

Ernie Corrigan

Joe Costello

Dick Crino

Luise Cahill Dittrich

Anne Barrett Doyle

Mike Emerton

Bill Fallon

Cathy Fallon

Joe Finn

Lynn Finn

Maureen Foley

Scott Fraser,
     Treasurer

Svea Fraser

John Gary

Andrea Johnson

Susan Jordan

Mary Ann Keyes

Steven Krueger,
     Executive Director

Jan Leary

Frank McConville

Julie McConville

Terry McKiernan

Kathy Mullaney

Maura O'Brien

Jeannette Post

Jim Post

Mary Scanlon

Midge Seibert

Bill Sheehan

Tom Smith

Rob Szpila

Peggie Thorp

Debby Tomazewski

Susan Troy

Ann Urban

Tom White

And to all those who will fulfill the potential of Voice of the Faithful to change the church.

CONTENTS

KEEP

THE

FAITH,

CHANGE

THE

CHURCH

CHAPTER 1

A CHURCH
OF GOOD AND EVIL

BISHOP WALTER EDYVEAN SAT directly in front of me across an enormous conference table in the wood-paneled boardroom of the Roman Catholic Archdiocese of Boston. Over his shoulder, just beyond a huge picture window, an encampment of journalists had maintained a vigil ever since the horrific news broke about the sexual abuse of children by priests and the cover-up by the church hierarchy. The almost-daily revelations of new atrocities, first in the *Boston Globe* and then in papers across the country, shocked Catholics every-where. The leaders of an institution dedicated to promoting Christian values had desecrated those values. It was as if fire-fighters had become arsonists, or doctors had intentionally spread disease.

The cover-up of sexual abuse by the hierarchy had caused me to question the foundation of my cultural and spiritual identity. The Catholic Church had guided and nurtured me in many ways. I was a graduate of St. Joan of Arc Grade School, Cathedral High School, and the University of Notre Dame before attending the Johns Hopkins Medical School. An uncle was a priest, an aunt a nun. My father had been the medical director of a large Catholic hospital. I had given commencement addresses at Catholic institutions and served on their academic committees.

I realized how enraged I truly felt one morning when I looked at the eighteen-inch-high Steuben cut-glass award on my desk. It had been presented to me by the Archbishop of Indianapolis, an award for my work to help prevent nuclear war. I read the inscription: "For your considerable impact on and service to our community." I noted the engraving at the top, CELEBRATING CATHOLIC SCHOOL VALUES, with the *T* of "Celebrating" in the form of a cross, and I recalled the great pride with which I had received the award. Yet in the immediate wake of the revelations I felt an urge to seize it, to smash it, to shatter it.

The scandal had actually caused me to consider leaving the church, or, as I would later express it, to acknowledge that the church, by its actions, had left *me*. But I could not leave the Catholic Church. It was the church into which I had been baptized as an infant, the church which had provided spiritual guidance throughout my life. It had done incalculable good for millions of others working for world peace, caring for the poor and sick, educating tens of millions of students throughout the world, working for world peace, nurturing countless souls across the millennia. It was the church of my beloved wife; the church of my parents and grandparents; the church in which my children had been raised. It was *my* church, and I could not leave it.

But I also knew that I could not remain and simply accept what had happened.

And so I helped form a grassroots organization called Voice of the Faithful. We are a group of devout Catholics, now more than thirty thousand strong, with a determination to be heard. We started out meeting in a suburban church basement and now have nearly two hundred active affiliates from Florida to Alaska. We are mainstream practicing Catholics, the lifeblood of our faith—parents and grandparents, Sunday school teachers, deacons, members of the choir, Eucharistic Ministers, and concerned members of our communities. We are hardly a band of radicals.

But while we are faithful Catholics, we are certain that if the laity had a meaningful role within the church, the sex abuse of children by priests would have been halted in its earliest stages. With lay people involved in the decision making, certainly no priest who had abused a child would have been transferred to another parish and allowed to molest other children—parents would never have permitted it.

Early on, then, the founding members of Voice of the Faithful decided that our historical docility had contributed to the cover-up and must end. We saw our meeting with Bishop Edyvean as a crucial step toward that goal. On the day of our meeting—May 23, 2002—we wanted to be embraced by the hierarchy, to work in partnership with them. Our goal was to forge a trusting relationship with the cardinal and others in the hierarchy so that the laity could gain a seat at the table, become part of the process of decision making, and help build a better church.

As Vicar General and moderator of the curia, second in command to Cardinal Bernard Law, Bishop Edyvean was a powerful figure. Now in his early sixties, he had a reputation as an erudite, courteous man who was particularly well connected, having served for some years at the Vatican. In Boston he played a behind-the-scenes role, implementing the policies of Cardinal Law.

Bishop Edyvean was joined by another priest, a young canon lawyer, while I was attending the meeting with two other members of our group, Mary Scanlon and Steve Krueger. I arrived just as the meeting was starting, having raced to the chancery from Massachusetts General Hospital, where I work as a cardiologist.

Coming to the meeting that day, I believed that we had much to offer the hierarchy. I felt a sense of exuberance for I knew we could help. I was sure that if the local hierarchy were to embrace us it would be a signal to countless Catholics deeply troubled by the scandal that there was a genuine desire to work with the laity to improve the Church. My excitement approaching the meeting was tempered, however, by reports we had been hearing that Bishop Edyvean was working back channels against us, presumably at Cardinal Law's instruction.

We began the meeting with a prayer, led by the bishop, and then exchanged pleasantries. Having been awarded honorary degrees from five Catholic colleges, I was accustomed to affable discussions with church officials, and I hoped this meeting would not be an exception. But the mood quickly grew tense as the younger priest, Father Mark O'Connell, attacked our group, claiming that our very existence somehow undermined the leadership of Cardinal Law.

While I was surprised by his arrogance, and the hostile tone he had suddenly injected into the meeting, I replied that we supported the authority of the hierarchy but that as lay Catholics we had a right and even a responsibility to help our church in its time of crisis.

Cardinal Law and other members of the hierarchy had committed grave errors of judgment transferring many priests who had sexually molested children to other parishes where they continued as sexual predators. The Cardinal had not only transferred these men, but he had led a massive cover-up as well. We noted that our group had been formed in response to these failures of the hierarchy.

The accusatory tone set by Father O'Connell made it easier for us to pose the difficult question for which we needed an answer.

"Bishop Edyvean," I said, "we've heard that you're blocking us in parishes, that you're calling pastors and telling them not to let Voice of the Faithful meet on church property." I looked him in the eye and paused a moment, then asked him directly: "Are you blocking us?"

The bishop hesitated, then replied, "There are a lot of issues we have with your organization. We have to know what you're about."

This response didn't ring true, for I was certain he already knew a great deal about us. A priest supportive of Voice had told us that Bishop Edyvean had downloaded materials from our Web site. Newspapers, magazines, and television networks from all over the world had reported on our movement. It was clear that we were about responding to the horrific sex abuse scandal to support victims whose lives had been so deeply scarred. We were about getting involved in the church so that never again would the culture of secrecy be permitted to cover up abuse of children and criminality. We were about using the talents and experience of educated, successful lay people—doctors, lawyers, professors, judges, business people, mothers, fathers—to help revive our church after the abuse scandal and assist in resolution of the many other problems of the Catholic Church. What Bishop Edyvean did not know about Voice of the Faithful from the many public sources was easily available from talking with us. We had no secrets. But we had been told that he acted against us before joining in dialogue.

As I looked across the table it was clear to me that Bishop Edyvean hoped I would drop the subject. But I couldn't. So I posed the question again, this time in a tone with a bit more intensity.

"Bishop Edyvean, are you trying to block us?" The tension in the room increased. The canon lawyer at the bishop's side frowned, clearly annoyed.

"We'll have to do more research," he said, continuing to evade the issue.

I replied as respectfully yet as directly as I could. "You haven't answered my question."

This was not easy for me. I was a sixty-year-old lifelong Catholic with an instinctive reverence for priests and bishops— indeed, for all church leaders. Yet I was also a scientist who believed in a probing search for the truth.

"Are you actively blocking our organization?"

There was a brittle silence.

Finally, Bishop Edyvean conceded that, yes, he had tried to block us, but he said that he had phoned only one parish.

While I appreciated his acknowledging an unpleasant truth, I was astonished that a bishop would act *against* some of the most enthusiastic Catholics in his archdiocese who were acting in compliance with all the rules of the church.

"We're concerned," he said.

Concerned? I thought. Concerned about mainstream lay Catholics who want to help their church through a crisis? I feared that the bishop's concern was reflective of what had gotten our church into trouble in the first place: a concern more for protecting the age-old culture of secrecy, for placing the power of the hierarchy above the safety of children.

Rather than pushing us away, rather than secretly trying to block our growth, it was clear to me that church leaders should have been doing the opposite—embracing us, welcoming our offers of help and support.

—∞—

As others at the table spoke, I thought back to my meeting with the hierarchy twenty-one years earlier in this very same conference room. The contrast in tone was striking. In 1981, the pastor of my church had helped me arrange a meeting with Cardinal Humberto Medeiros, the predecessor to Cardinal Law. At that time the United States and the Soviet Union were engaged in mad rhetoric about winning a nuclear war. Having worked in the Soviet Union as a young physician, I had gotten to know a number of Russian doctors, including Dr. Evgeny Chazov, an esteemed cardiologist who included among his patients Soviet president Leonid Brezhnev. Along with my American colleagues Drs. Bernard Lown, Eric Chivian, and Dr. John Pastore, I joined with the Russians to form a group called International Physicians for the Prevention of Nuclear War. Our goal was to frame the nuclear debate in medical terms, to educate people throughout the world that any sort of nuclear exchange would be a medical catastrophe. We believed that accurately describing the medical consequences of nuclear war would convince the people of the world to force their political leaders to move beyond the bellicose language of the Cold War.

Early on in our antinuclear efforts, we were criticized as being naive dupes of the Soviet propaganda machine. If this charge were to stick it would have severely damaged our movement. I realized that nothing would combat that charge more effectively than if Pope John Paul II, with his impeccable anti-Communist credentials, were to endorse our group. I had sought the meeting with Cardinal Medeiros, to ask whether he would help our organization obtain a letter of support from the Holy Father. This was a highly unusual request. It was not common for the Vatican to send out letters on request, but Cardinal Medeiros supported our mission and agreed to help. I told the cardinal that there was some urgency in my request—our group planned its first convention in just six weeks.

He asked what I hoped the Holy Father might say in his letter, and I volunteered to draft something. He readily agreed, and I set about doing so—right there at the very table where I was to meet with Bishop Edyvean. As I wrote, Cardinal Medeiros brought me several documents from his office containing the Pope's statements on nuclear war, pointing out a wonderful excerpt from the encyclical *Pacem in Terris*, issued by Pope John XXIII, "on establishing universal peace in truth, justice, charity and liberty."

Six weeks later, at the first conference of International Physicians for the Prevention of Nuclear War, in Washington, D.C., a letter arrived from Pope John Paul II endorsing our efforts. It was a crucial statement by the church at the ideal time—a prime example of the Catholic Church using its moral authority to bring the teachings of Christ to the modern world. The Pope's endorsement helped us build an international organization with 130,000 physicians in more than twenty nations, which in turn led to a massive grassroots uprising that altered the discussion of nuclear war. President Reagan sent us a statement at a later conference indicating that, "Nuclear war cannot be won and must never be fought."

Five years after we received the letter from the Holy Father, I traveled to Oslo, where our group was awarded the Nobel Peace Prize.

This had been the church at its best. But now we were confronting the church at its worst. Shadowing our meeting with Bishop Edyvean were the unspeakable crimes that had been committed by priests and covered up by the hierarchy. Father John Geoghan alone, it is believed, molested more than 130 children in a half-dozen parishes over three decades. He had fondled some, raped others, traumatized all. After abusing a twelve-year-old boy whose father had recently committed suicide, Geoghan told the child to keep it secret. "We're very good at keeping secrets," the priest told him.

Cardinal Law, and even Cardinal Medeiros, despite knowing of Father Geoghan's crimes, wrote glowing letters for this sexual predator as they assigned him to new parishes. And then there was the matter of Father Ronald H. Paquin openly admitting his transgressions to a *Boston Globe* reporter. "Sure, I fooled around. But I never raped anyone and I never felt gratified myself," the priest said. There was a case where both a father and his son had been molested by priests a generation apart. And there was the shocking story of Father Paul Shanley, who reportedly left a trail of sodomy and ruin in his wake.

These horrific crimes—and the many others that have been reported since—have made it clear that, like a decubitus skin ulceration, the decay of the Catholic Church was deeper and broader than the surface signs indicated.

When we first explored ways that Voice of the Faithful might help our church, we were told by some that lay people, who represent 99.9 percent of the church, should simply acquiesce to mandates from the hierarchy. But we quickly learned that in the early 1960s, the historic Vatican II ecumenical council had called for the laity to actively participate in the leadership of the church. And as we reached back thousands of years before Vatican II to the roots of our religion—to the words and life of Christ—we also found our faith strengthened. We realized that during this early period, the laity was the church. The church did not start with an imperial style. On the contrary, when Christ himself was alive on this earth and could have acted as an autocratic ruler, he preached and lived a message of humility, love, and inclusiveness far different from that modeled by some current members of the hierarchy. The statement by Christ that Peter was the rock upon which the church would be built is often cited as support for a strong central authority, but Christ also advocated many of the principles of respect for individuals underlying modern democratic structures.

This notion strikes some as radical because the mantra that "The Church is not a democracy" has been repeated so many times. Our first response to this criticism was to make it clear that we did not intend to vote on the core beliefs of the faith—these we accepted. We would, however, debate and vote on the manner in which the church operates. Our study of church governance revealed that even in the present church there are many democratic practices such as the selection of a pope by voting and the debate and voting on resolutions at conferences of bishops. Over time, though, the laity have become disenfranchised, a problem we intended to correct.

As the meeting with Bishop Edyvean and Father O'Connell drew to a close, I proposed that we agree on a joint statement we would make to the press. In the spirit of conciliation, I suggested, and Bishop Edyvean agreed, that we say we had a productive meeting and would meet again.

As I left the room, I realized that before the news of the sexual abuse and cover-up had been revealed, the hierarchy surely could have secretly spread the word that they wanted a group like ours suppressed, barred from meeting in various parishes, and it would have been done. But the scandal had changed everything. There were now thousands of lay people demanding that the flaws that led to the sexual abuse cover-up, and other problems, be corrected. The faithful now realized that the scandal was a symptom of the underlying problem of unbalanced power in the hands of fallible humans—a flawed structure that had led to the cover-up and many other problems of the Roman Catholic Church in the twentieth century.

The primary effect of the abuse and cover-up has been extraordinary harm to survivors. But in stepping forward, these brave witnesses revealed the flaws of the church and generated the energy in the laity that might help correct the underlying problem. In addition to the laity becoming active, hundreds of parish priests were also calling for change, as were theologians. Cardinal Law and his associates could try to stop our movement; they could try to stop the laity from organizing. But as we left the meeting, I knew that they would fail. The time had arrived for the voice of the faithful to be heard.

CHAPTER 2

A NEW VOICE FOR THE FAITHFUL EMERGES

— I —

THE PATH TO THE DIFFICULT MEETING with Bishop Edyvean began months earlier with the shocking revelations by the *Boston Globe* of massive abuse of children by priests and cover-up by the hierarchy. My wife, Kathleen, and I, parishioners at St. John the Evangelist parish in Wellesley, a Boston suburb, struggled to understand how we might respond. We finally decided that I should ask our pastor, Father Tom Powers, if the laity could hold a discussion group on the topic.

On the first Sunday in February of 2002, I waited in the vestibule after mass for the congregation to leave so that I could talk with Father Powers. I saw John and Mary Riley, the proud parents of a priest and my friends of many years. We talked about the revelations and it was clear that they too were greatly affected by the scandal.

"I'm going to ask Father Tom if we can start a discussion group," I told them. "If you think it makes sense, perhaps you could join me in the request?"

So John, Mary, and I approached Father Tom. "Would it be possible," I asked him, "to hold a meeting in the church hall so that the parishioners can talk about this? It might work best if the meeting be led by a member of the laity, and I would be willing to do that."

John added that he had heard me lead group discussions many years ago during the peace movement and that I could probably do it well.

In a considered and thoughtful manner, Father Tom replied, "It sounds like a good idea, but I'd like to think it over and consult with others. I'll give you a call."

After mulling it over for a couple of days, Father Tom called me and offered us a meeting place on Monday nights. He also suggested that we invite anyone who wanted to discuss the scandal to remain in the pews after mass.

The following Sunday, Kathleen and I went to the eleven o'clock mass at St. John's—a mass as routine as the hundreds we had attended there over thirty years. Looking over the congregation of about two hundred, I saw many old friends. I saw

Svea Fraser, a deeply religious woman with an intense commitment to the church, attending mass with her husband, Scott. I would learn that Svea was struggling with the crisis by deepening her already extensive religious study. She had been particularly struck by a passage from the spiritual writer Carlo Carretto that she had encountered in *The Holy Longing* by Ronald Rolheiser. Even though Carretto wrote the piece years before the current crisis, Svea had found it so apt that she copied it down and carried it with her in her purse.

Either by coincidence or the hand of the Holy Spirit, Father Tom had selected the identical Carretto reading as the basis for his homily. As he prepared to read the excerpt, Father Tom told us: "People don't leave failing institutions, they leave failing institutions that don't change." And then he read the excerpt.

> *How much I must criticize you, my church and yet*
> *how much I love you! You have made me suffer more*
> *than anyone and yet I owe more to you than to anyone.*
> *I should like to see you destroyed and yet I need your*
> *presence. You have given me much scandal and yet you*
> *alone have made me understand holiness. Never in this*
> *world have I seen anything more compromised, more*
> *false, yet never have I touched anything more pure,*
> *more generous or more beautiful.*
>
>   *Countless times I have felt like slamming the door*
> *of my soul in your face—and yet, every night, I have*

prayed that I might die in your sure arms! No, I cannot be free of you, for I am one with you, even if not completely you. Then too—where would I go? To build another church? But I could not build one without the same defects, for they are my defects. And again, if I were to build another church, it would be my church, not Christ's church. No. I am old enough. I know better!

When the mass ended, Father Powers announced that there would be a discussion of the crisis for those who wished to stay. He encouraged us to use our voices. While some parishioners began to file out, it became clear that many others wanted to talk—almost a third of the congregation remained in the pews. Some who had been in pews in the back moved closer to the front. As agreed in advance, another parishioner named Tom Smith and I went to the front, between the congregation and the altar, and Father Powers handed me the microphone.

"I want to thank Father Powers for giving us this opportunity to discuss the terrible crisis in our church," I began. "I have found it very confusing and distressing. I suspect many of you feel the same way. We thought it might be useful to share our reactions to the revelations that are occurring."

Father Powers, in the vestments he had worn for the mass, sat off to the side, listening. I looked around at the group, hoping that someone would speak. There was silence for a long moment and with it came an air of tension.

The quiet voice of a woman broke the silence. As she started to speak, she faltered and a hush fell over the group. She was trembling and suddenly tears were streaming down her face. She started sobbing audibly, and as she did so she said: "I don't know what to tell my children."

There was a stunned silence, an air of reverence that greeted her words, for she seemed to embody it all—the overwhelming emotion of it, the confusion, the terrible hurt.

Emboldened by the woman, several others spoke and they, too, were visibly shaken. Luise Cahill Dittrich rose. She was smart—a fast talker and clear thinker. When she had first heard about the abuse scandal she had thought, "This could have been my son." She thought about the children whose lives had been ruined and she grew angry.

"If women were involved this would never have happened," Luise urgently told the group. "This is what happens when you don't have women involved, when you don't have married people involved."

The woman behind Luise began crying. She talked about two priests who had been accused of molestation. She said she had had them as guests in her home for dinner. Another woman who was raising her children Catholic wondered how she could justify this to her husband, who was of another faith.

Peggie Thorp, a lifelong Catholic, was nearly too nervous to speak, but she was far too angry *not* to speak. Peggie is a writer, the mother of three grown daughters. She welcomed the session; she had found herself talking to fellow parishioners after mass for weeks, talking in hushed tones. I did not know Peggie at the time, but after she was finished speaking, no one there would forget her. As she spoke, her voice was shaking with fury. "I share the same outrage that everyone else has expressed this morning, but I do think something like this was bound to happen. This is an institution that has operated for fifteen hundred years on only half of its strength, the male half."

Jim Post, with his neatly combed black hair and trimmed mustache, sat taking all this in. Jim is a business school professor and lawyer in his late fifties. During the course of the mass, he had been thinking about the litany of saints referenced in the liturgy. They didn't get there by living in good times, he thought. They lived in times when they were challenged to stand up for something. He thought, maybe this is our time to stand up.

When Jim spoke, he likened the archdiocesan cover-up to scandals in the business world—to Enron and other companies that had deceived stockholders and employees. And then he quoted Justice Brandeis: "Sunlight," he said, "is the best disinfectant."

Svea Fraser agreed and reflected on what the co-leader of the discussion, Tom Smith, had said. Someone lamented that these were dark days for the church, but Tom, who was studying to become a church deacon, had disagreed—he said that the darkest days were when we didn't know.

Someone likened the current crisis to the perfect storm in which a number of atmospheric elements collide to create a rare and violent upheaval. In modern Catholicism there had long been powerful undercurrents of dissent on issues such as women's ordination, divorce, and birth control, and now, on top of it all, came the abuse of innocents and a cover-up by the hierarchy. Svea stood and said that the church is all of us, not just the bishops. She said that the crisis was not one of faith but of flawed leadership.

Susan Scully Troy, like Svea, held a master's in divinity degree. She observed that many had lost the sense of security the church had provided. People were questioning whether they had been too trusting.

After about twenty people had spoken, we ended the session, but it was clear that we had tapped into an enormous well of emotion and opinion. I announced that there would be another meeting the next night in the church basement for those who wished to continue the dialogue.

—II—

On Monday night, as we drove to St. John's, Kathleen and I wondered whether anyone would show up. We arrived a few minutes early and were disappointed to find that the parking lot was empty. We walked over to the darkened social hall in the basement of the church. Within just a few minutes, however, several dozen people arrived, bringing life to the room.

The steel folding chairs were arranged in rows facing the

front of the room where there was a small stage. I knew the arrangement was wrong. This was not a time for listening to an announcement from a church leader. The people of the church needed to talk to and hear one another as equals. I suggested that we rearrange the chairs to form a large circle. The circle complete, we took our seats, including Father Powers, who told us he was there to listen.

We opened the meeting with a brief prayer and then I suggested that we simply go around the circle, have people identify themselves, say how long they'd been at St. John's, and offer whatever comments they'd like. Peggie Thorp, who led the session with me, agreed with this plan.

An older man who I knew to be devout and conservative in his Catholicism was red-faced with anger. He said that he had trusted too much. He said he had raised all of his children Catholic and now he was embarrassed in front of them.

One woman sat silently for a long moment, then said: "I just wanted to see your faces. I wanted to be with a community of Catholics."

A middle-aged couple talked about their son. They said they had never spoken publicly before but wanted to do so now. And so they spoke, in subdued tones, choked with emotion, about their child who had been sexually molested by a priest in whom they had placed their trust. As he listened, Jim Post felt as though he had been kicked in the stomach. He sat there thinking, "The pain this has caused them and their child—a child we *knew*."

A retired high school principal in his sixties was a lifelong Catholic and the father of five sons. For a time, he had been a member of St. Julia's parish in Weston, the next town over from Wellesley and one of the parishes where Father John Geoghan had abused children. This man was furious. He said that if this had happened in one of the schools where he had been a principal, the offender would have been gone by nightfall. And then he wondered aloud whether he had been too trusting; whether he had placed too much faith in the church; whether he had been "too Catholic." He wondered whether he had failed to listen attentively enough to any of his sons. He wondered whether one of his boys had ever tried to tell him anything. Was it possible one of his boys *had* tried to broach the subject with him and he had somehow shut him out? We shared his sense of betrayal when he said, "I never believed a priest would do this."

An older woman talked about growing up in a Catholic family and her conviction that "if I had said, 'Father touched me inappropriately,' I know I would not be believed and Father would be believed. My mother would have hit me if I'd said anything bad about Father."

People nodded, knowing that their trust—*our* trust—in priests had been absolute.

A woman spoke about two of her nephews who had been sexually abused. She thought it had never happened to anyone else.

Fighting back tears, Mary Scanlon said, "My first thought was for the victims, for the children who had spent their youth and adulthood carrying this terrible burden. It contaminated their whole lives." She was so disturbed by their stolen innocence that she felt compelled to find them, to share their sorrow, and to work with them to find a way to heal. "I'm a parent," she said. "What is more fundamental to our Catholic heritage than the image of the relationship between the Father and the Son? For a parent, the child is the ultimate sign of faith, hope, and love. The child believes that what the parent says is true, trusts that he will be cared for, and loves the parent with boundless devotion. We, as parents, don't just talk about this. We live it. If we fall short, our family relationships break down and we see the evidence all over the place, then we have to fix it. Parents know this at a gut level."

There was tension in the room; a sense that things were being said aloud that had never been said before—certainly not in this setting. Perhaps as much as anything else, there was a sense of confusion. How could our church have done this? people wondered aloud. How could this possibly have happened?

As I listened to the passionate and deeply insightful comments that were emerging from the discussions, I sensed that the common sense of a small group of ordinary people in dialogue was creating a powerful message of value for millions. I recognized it as similar to the moment when a small group of Russian and American physicians formulated what led to a worldwide organization.

Thinking of the path ahead, I expected that at some point we might find ourselves in confrontation with some members of the hierarchy. I turned to Father Powers, who had been sitting quietly as a member of the circle. He had passed when the opportunity to speak reached his place, but he had been greatly moved by the faith of those who had spoken.

"Father Tom," I said, "there may come a time when we make a statement, or take some action, that could cause difficulty for you. Perhaps it would be better if our future meetings were not held on the premises of St. John's Church." I said this partly to protect Father Tom from harm, but also to provide us with the freedom we might need to act.

I was struck by the depth and simplicity of his response: "Of course you should continue to meet here. You *are* the Church."

It had taken us more than two hours to work our way completely around the circle. Everyone had spoken.

As difficult as it had been, Susan Troy felt that "it was a graced moment. There was a palpable feeling of the movement of the Spirit, of being in the presence of God. We were being moved to speak. We needed to not let the anger go. We were being told to act, to do something."

My feelings after the meeting are best described by the famous prayer of Thomas Merton, the Trappist monk, whose hermitage in Kentucky I once visited:

> *My Lord God, I have no idea where I'm going. I do not see the road ahead of me. I cannot know for certain where it will end. Nor do I really know myself*

and the fact that I think I am following your will does
not mean I am actually doing so.

But I believe that the desire to please you does in
fact please you. I hope that I will never do anything
apart from that desire. And I know that if I do this
you will lead me by the right road though I may know
nothing about it . . . .

I will not fear, for you are ever with me.

We left the meeting not sure of what lay ahead, but we knew the journey had begun.

— III —

The following Monday night I asked Susan Troy, whom I learned had a gift for liturgy, to lead us in an opening prayer. The size of our group had increased from forty to about sixty. New arrivals said they had heard something special was happening in the basement of St. John's and they wanted to be part of it. We needed an easy way for them to join us. Through my work at the hospital, I had seen an effective way to welcome newcomers. Dr. John Parrish, director of the Center for the Integration of Medicine and Innovative Technology, asks each new person at our weekly forum to explain their reason for coming. We borrowed Dr. Parrish's method and it became our standard way of opening our meetings. The newcomers expressed many thoughts similar to those we had spoken of the week before—shock, anger, love of the Catholic faith.

While a consistent picture of the scandal began to emerge and all felt supported by the common understanding, we were not sure where to go—not sure of our purpose. Ever so slowly, the group began the difficult process of turning our energies from emotion to intellect. While we felt a continued need to talk, a powerful desire to learn and to *act* began to emerge. When we started discussing issues such as pedophilia, ephebophilia, and the structure of the church hierarchy, we quickly realized the breadth and depth of our ignorance.

"We were at ground zero of understanding about these things," said Jim Post. "But when you put a group of successful people around a table they're going to begin to take apart the problem."

And that's what was happening. There were Svea Fraser and Susan Troy, two bright women each of whom possessed a master's of divinity degree; Svea's husband, Scott, a Harvard Business School graduate and business consultant; Jim Post, a professor who possessed an MBA, a Ph.D., *and* a law degree; Peggie Thorp was taking time away from her writing projects; Mary Scanlon, a nurse practitioner and social services counselor; Paul Baier, a young dot.com entrepreneur and another Harvard Business School grad. Bill Fallon was an accomplished retired businessman, his wife, Cathy, an official at Brandeis University.

In the months to come, there would be literally hundreds of others from all walks of life who would bring their talents and devotion to work for a better church. It was—and remains to this day—one of the most impressive collaborative efforts I have ever been part of. These were gifted, devoted Catholics—all of whom would go on to play pivotal roles in Voice of the Faithful.

Somehow in the gathering that evening, Svea Fraser stood out. Slender, in her early fifties, with a ready smile, a warm manner, and an intense combination of intellect and spirituality, the French newspaper *Le Figaro* would later describe her as "une elegante cinquantine"—elegant in her fifties. She had grown up in Connecticut, the oldest of ten children, two of whom had died in infancy—one when Svea was twelve, the other when she was fourteen. These terrible losses had profoundly impacted on Svea, intensifying a belief within her that there was a deeper meaning to existence.

Few Catholics I knew had devoted the time and energy to their faith that Svea had. During the 1970s her husband Scott had been in business school. At the time, Svea started thinking about pursuing theological studies at Andover Newton Theological School. At the time she was also an integral participant in St. John's parish and friends with Father Philbin, the pastor who preceded Father Powers. Svea would sometimes talk with Father Philbin about her desire to enrich her spiritual education, and one day the pastor came to her with exciting news: Cardinal Law had said that Svea could be admitted to study at the Pope John XXIII Seminary in Weston. This seminary was devoted to those who had decided later in life that they were called to the priesthood. On the first day of classes Svea found herself in a classroom full of men, including two Trappist monks. Her two girls started calling her the Church Lady, after one of the zany characters on the television show *Saturday Night Live*. Svea and Scott laughed along with the girls at the humor, but the truth was that the church lady was in her element at the seminary. She studied hard and in 1989 graduated with a master's in divinity. Every other person in her graduating class was ordained a priest in the Roman Catholic Church.

While Svea was barred by church rules from becoming a priest, there were many other ways in which she could use her training. Not long after graduation she was invited by the cardinal to serve on several archdiocesan policy committees. She was also hired as the first female Catholic assistant chaplain at Wellesley College.

On Monday evening she had walked into the church basement unsure what to expect. She knew that American Catholics in general were a docile lot, having long been content to pray, pay, and obey. But she also knew that because this crisis involved the violation of children that it would "get parents catapulted out of the pew." To me, Svea symbolized the best of the Catholic laity. She was no rebel. She was a woman with the depth and intensity of commitment who loved her church and who wanted to do something to help it.

— I V —

Over the next several weeks we made progress in identifying our common purpose and goals. As we learned more about the sexual abuse incidents and their effects, we became certain that we would make a major effort to support the victims—or, as we were learning they were more appropriately called, *survivors*. Mary Scanlon and Jeannette Post, a physician and the spouse of Jim Post, led our working group on survivors. They both urged that our number one goal should be to support survivors; all agreed.

In our discussions it became clear that we all loved the church at least in part because most had had wonderful experiences through the years with various priests. In just about every case, a priest—and often more than one—had played a central, positive role in someone's life. Many of these priests were now victims of prejudice and suspicion because of the actions of a relatively small number of predators, and because of the failure of the system of oversight. So we adopted a second goal of providing support for priests of integrity.

And we began to realize that the sexual abuse scandal was a symptom of a deeper problem. We did not yet know our role in addressing this structural problem of the church, but we sensed that the limited, passive role of the laity must come to an end.

And then, as though receiving manna from above, we were given an answer as to what our next step should be. Ironically, the guidance came from Cardinal Bernard Law himself. For a decade,

Cardinal Law had hosted an annual convocation of several thousand laity who were most active in the programs of the archdiocese. The meetings included priests and lay people from each parish. This year's meeting was just a couple of weeks away. Cardinal Law had made a decision at the urging of a number of parish priests to discard the planned agenda and turn the meeting into what the archdiocese was calling a listening session. The idea was for the Cardinal and his bishops to give lay people an opportunity to speak candidly about the crisis—he would listen, and move forward informed by the thoughts of the faithful.

The timing and the format of the event were perfect for us. A listening session gave us a goal and imposed a deadline that required discipline and focus. We felt we had much to say. We would use the opportunity of the convocation to speak clearly and forcefully to the hierarchy; we would state our views and we would extend our hand to help the cardinal lead our church through the crisis. It would be a defining moment for our newly developing group. We were thrilled with the opportunity.

The optimists in our group interpreted the plans of the Cardinal for the listening session as a positive sign. The plan for the convocation suggested that Cardinal Law was reaching out, that he wanted to listen and seek ideas—that he knew he *needed* help.

Even those more pessimistic about the Cardinal's intentions, who did not think that "listening" would be useful, if it were to occur, saw the convocation as a means to reach out beyond St. John's to other Catholics in the more than three hundred parishes of the archdiocese. Most Catholics are closely connected to their own parish and have very little contact with Catholics in other parishes. We knew we were isolated, and we already sensed we were dealing with issues that could only be addressed on a larger scale. I thought there was a chance that the same small flame that had ignited at St. John's could also spark action in other parishes.

And so we began to plan for the convocation.

"We decided that if we were going to go to the convocation we would want to say something well thought out," said Mary Scanlon. "We did not intend to be casual about this." We all wanted a respectful, positive document that could build on any cooperative actions the Cardinal and the hierarchy might take.

I sent an e-mail to Peggie Thorp suggesting that "we should have a document . . . that could be read by someone (not me) to the convocation. The most important message would be to encourage discussion in all three hundred parishes." I wrote a rough original draft, which Peggie took and, working with others, fashioned into a clear statement of what we were about.

The convocation was an invitation-only event. We learned from Father Tom that our parish was allotted a dozen seats. He told us that all twelve could go to our group, if we wanted them. We, of course, accepted. The Monday night before the Saturday convocation, we met to discuss our statement.

We also knew we needed a name. Catholics for Renewal or Catholics for Reform had been suggested, but several of us noted that both *renewal* and *reform* were code words for prior movements that had polarized, and paralyzed, the laity. We sensed we were something different.

Svea Fraser had introduced us to the concept of *sensus fidelium*, or sense of the faithful, articulated in the documents of Vatican II. The term refers to the idea that the faithful when acting together as a result of careful discernment will be guided by the Holy Spirit. The profound, unified expressions of faith we had developed in our meetings left me with little doubt that we embodied this "sense of the faithful." The term seemed right.

Since we were expressing the *sensus fidelium*, Scott Fraser suggested we call ourselves Vox Fidelium. But Susan Troy, who had heard more than enough Latin while studying for her divinity degree, thought that the term would be associated with the secret methods and autocratic style we were trying to change. Susan said Latin was the language of the institutional church and that as a lay organization we should use English, the vernacular welcomed by Vatican II. Thus was our two-month-old organization christened Voice of the Faithful.

Just a few days later, after a good deal of review, our group agreed upon a statement to present at the convocation. The next day, we developed an electronic means to share this document with the world. Paul Baier, one of our younger members, had used his dot.com experience to put a simple Web site together where he posted our statement. Although few were listening at that early moment, the Voice of the Faithful could now be heard throughout the world.

CHAPTER 3

THE CARDINAL CONVENES HIS FLOCK

—I—

SHORTLY AFTER 7 O'CLOCK on Saturday morning, March 9, I drove to St. John's to meet the other members of the group of twelve who would represent Voice of the Faithful in its first venture out of the parish. The day was cool and overcast, the impressive white steeple set against a leaden gray sky. As I pulled into the school parking lot, I saw the women in our group were all wearing bright red. They had chosen this as a sign of the Pentecostal spirit.

We gathered in a small circle for a last-minute review of strategy—it reminded me of a team huddle before an important game. Svea Fraser, Mary Scanlon, Susan Troy, Kathi Aldridge, Paul Baier, Luise Dittrich, Andrea Johnson, Maura and John O'Brien, Jeannette Post, and Peggie Thorp—all of us now tightly bonded in a common purpose. Susan Troy led us in a prayer seeking the help of the Holy Spirit. Then we split up into groups and headed east into Boston, encountering only minimal traffic at this early hour.

The World Trade Center is a massive structure on the South Boston waterfront that looks out on Boston Harbor and across the water to Logan Airport. I rode with Mary Scanlon and we arrived to find thousands of people pulling into the parking facilities across the street. With numerous TV satellite trucks lined up outside the building, I had the feeling I was going to a major sporting event—as though the Bruins had made the playoffs.

To get into the Trade Center we had to walk by a gauntlet of protesters wielding signs, guitars, and bullhorns. Adding to the raucous atmosphere were contingents of media and police—it was the wildest scene I had ever encountered at a religious meeting. I felt a strong sense of kinship with the picketers. The victims among them—the survivors—had been treated so badly that I believed they had every right to be out there picketing. I didn't want to rush past them as a privileged insider, so I took the time to walk along the sidewalk and read their signs. Some called for the Cardinal's resignation, others condemned the entire church. JUSTICE AND MERCY FOR VICTIMS, SPEAKING OUT IS HOLY, and SHAME.

Among those taking part in the protest was Father Bill Kremmel, a priest whom I knew had been active in Pax Christi, a Catholic peace group. We spoke briefly. I told him we would be carrying the message inside.

As I walked among the other protesters, several glared at me as I showed my pass and was permitted to enter. The experience highlighted the different strategies that the protesters and our group had decided to use. Voice of the Faithful had made a conscious decision to work for change from within the church. It was the strategy we believed would mobilize the greatest number of people, and the approach that best suited our group. There had been some tension at our meetings over how forceful a presentation we should make and over tactics as well. And it had become clear that there was a reluctance among our members to engage in active protest.

Inside, past security, the main hall was massive enough to hold the three thousand Catholics who had arrived from more than three hundred parishes in Greater Boston. The crowd was well dressed, polite, and older—the good people who gave life to the church on a daily basis. I wondered if they shared the outrage of the protesters on the street.

We found seats toward the rear, so far back that the figures on the massive stage seemed remote. It was better to watch the proceedings on a large TV monitor off to the left.

As angry as we all were—and that was clearly a crucial element of the fuel that propelled us—we had arrived at the convocation with hope and great expectations. As soon as Peggie Thorp entered that cavernous space, she said she was reassured by these thousands of people; she felt the presence of the *sensus fidelium*. Svea believed that the Cardinal would be happy we did not want to leave the church, that we wanted to stay and be part of the solution. She thought he would think, "we have a problem here and we have educated laity committed to this. Let's look at a solution together." She thought of our message to the Cardinal as "we're your new best friends. We have something to bring to the table."

Paul Baier put into words a thought that many of us shared: "The Cardinal just doesn't realize how bad it is because he hasn't been a parent; we'll tell him and he'll understand."

While I believed that Cardinal Law had, to this point, handled the sex abuse situation very poorly, I too was hopeful that his initiative to organize this "listening" session was a sign that he would put those mistakes behind him. To me, his poor performance on the abuse issue was a paradox. Cardinal Law was a man with a powerful intellect and a record of accomplishment. He was a 1953 graduate of Harvard who was known through most of his career for progressive policies on a variety of social issues. After his ordination as a priest, young Father Law was assigned to a parish in Natchez, Mississippi, where he was an ardent civil rights activist. In the late 1960s he worked in Washington on improving relations between the Roman Catholic Church and Jews and Protestants. Appointed a bishop in 1973, he was assigned to the Springfield diocese in Missouri where he was again known for progressive policies—including opening the first home for battered women in Springfield. My father had worked with him on the formation of the Catholic Bioethics Center, which is now located in Boston

Bishop Law was chosen by Pope John Paul II as the Archbishop of Boston in the fall of 1983. The new archbishop soon became a strong public opponent of abortion rights. Elevated to cardinal in 1985, he became involved in a number of international issues. He led a Catholic-Jewish pilgrimage to Poland where the group visited Auschwitz and Catholic shrines. In 1996 he joined a White House protest urging President Clinton to support a proposal outlawing late-term abortions.

Within Greater Boston the cardinal was an immensely influential man. He counted among his friends and informal advisers many of the city's leading business, civic, and political leaders. But he had decried newspaper coverage of sexual abuse by priests—once even calling the "power of God on the media and especially" the *Boston Globe* for publishing such stories.

Nonetheless, given the recent revelations we thought he would now ask forgiveness and do what was right for the survivors.

After everyone was settled in their seats, we thought the listening would begin. It did—but we were the ones listening. The Cardinal, from the height of the stage, looked down and addressed his flock.

He began with a derisive comment about the media generally and the *Globe* in particular, and then struck a second discordant note by referring a number of times to "minors." All around us we could hear people in hushed tones repeat the word in disbelief.

"They're children," thought Paul Baier. "*Minors* is a lawyer's term."

On my way in I had been thinking, How could this be a genuine success? What would have to happen for this to go really well? And it was clear to me and I suspect to many others that the Cardinal would have to *hear what we are saying* and to act upon it. But even after Cardinal Law concluded his opening remarks, there was no time for listening. We sat and watched as the Cardinal, a group of bishops, and two dozen priests filed solemnly onto the stage and began celebrating an elaborate mass. The Cardinal wore his miter, the tall, formal hat that evoked medieval papal scenes. He walked with his crosier in his right hand. It was unsettling—on a day that demanded humility from the hierarchy. I watched the mass knowing that this man, resplendent in his opulent vestments, had personally approved the transfer of Father Geoghan.

I exchanged glances with others from our group who appeared to be having the same reaction. It seemed that the mass was being used as a way to force the laity—on a day that was supposed to be devoted to listening to their voices—to remain silent and docile.

Svea Fraser was fuming at the insensitivity of the proceedings. She was surprised that the mass had been scheduled at the beginning of the session rather than at the end of the day. She recalled the Scripture passage from Matthew 5:22–24, ". . . I say to you that everyone who is angry with his brother shall be liable to judgment . . . so if you are offering your gift at the altar, leave your gift there before the altar and go; first be reconciled to your brother, and then come and offer your gift." But there had not even been an attempt at reconciliation.

Also, still fresh in her mind was a scene from less than forty-eight hours earlier when she had attended a meeting of Archdiocesan Campus Ministers at Tufts University. The group of chaplains at twenty-two colleges and universities in the Greater Boston area met on a regular basis to discuss various issues. As assistant chaplain at Wellesley College, Svea went to the meeting with great excitement, eager to tell her colleagues in ministry about the Voice of the Faithful and the statement we would be making at the convocation. At the meeting, she distributed copies of our statement to the other chaplains, including the director of campus ministry for the archdiocese. Svea sat as her colleagues read the statement. She saw many heads nodding in agreement. Several congratulated her on it. But the director of campus ministry had a different reaction. She turned to Svea with a look of displeasure. In her zeal for this initiative, it had not occurred to Svea that it might not be welcomed by all. She remembered that it was the director's final remark that had a chilling effect on her.

"Just don't lose your head, Svea," she said sharply.

Now Svea sat listening intently during the mass. When the Gospel reading came, she was struck by the appropriateness of the message. It was from Luke, chapter 18, verses 9–14:

[Jesus] then spoke this parable addressed to those who believed in their own self-righteousness while holding everyone else in contempt. "Two men went up to the temple to pray. One was a Pharisee, the other a tax collector. The Pharisee, with head unbowed, prayed in this fashion: 'I give you thanks, oh God, that I am not like the rest of men grasping, crooked, adulteress—or even like this tax collector. I fast twice a week, I pay tithes on all I possess.' The other man, however, kept his distance not even daring to raise his eyes to heaven. All he did was beat his breast and say, 'Oh, God, be merciful to me, a sinner.' Believe me, this man went home from the temple justified but the other did not for everyone who exalts himself shall be humbled while he who humbles himself shall be exalted."

Svea couldn't believe how perfect the reading was! She quickly thumbed through her book to see whether this was the scheduled reading of the day or whether it had been chosen specifically for this occasion. She found that it was, in fact, the scheduled reading. How remarkable, she thought. Here was an ideal opportunity to talk about Phariseeism, for the Pharisees were the high priests, arrogant and aloof, sharply criticized by Jesus. Jesus said that they lorded it over others, that they were white on the outside but rotten on the inside. Svea thought what an ideal opportunity for the Cardinal to stand up and acknowledge failure. The Cardinal, however, did not take this path. Instead, he spoke of the Pharisees as being good men who struggled to find the right path.

"The mass was staged," complained Mary Scanlon. "We were snookered into being a big audience for the Cardinal's mass with the press looking on." It really bothered Mary that reporters were allowed into the mass but not the listening sessions. "We didn't want a show as though everything was okay, because everything was *not* okay."

Susan Troy couldn't help but notice that there were no lay readers, no lay Eucharistic Ministers involved in the mass. "I was upset at the Eucharist being used not for creating unity and communion at the end of the day, but as a platform for the Cardinal's spin at the beginning of the day," Susan said. Susan, Svea, Peggie, and Luise were so distressed by the event that they chose not to take communion.

— I I —

After the mass, the crowd of three thousand dispersed into a half-dozen listening sessions. One person from each parish was allowed to attend a special session with Cardinal Law. We had agreed in advance that Maura O'Brien would be our representative and that she would read our statement to the Cardinal. We wished her good luck.

The rest of us went off to a session with Bishop Lennon,

one of several bishops in the Boston Archdiocese. The meeting was held upstairs in a large rectangular room overlooking the harbor. We sat in rows of folding chairs facing the windows. Bishop Lennon sat with his back to the harbor, with several assistants facing us. There were two aisles and several microphones at which people could speak. Mary had rushed in and secured seats for all of us in a row right next to one of the microphones. About five hundred people filled the room.

The facilitator, a woman employed by the archdiocese, initiated the session and someone from the audience went to the microphone to make a comment. Mary nudged Peggie Thorp to get ready, and as soon as the other person was done, Peggie got up. She had led our group in drafting and revising our declaration, so the group chose her as the best person to read it. She stood tall and striking in her red dress, and read our statement in a sharp, clear voice:

"We are the Church," she began.

> We speak on behalf of a group of committed Catholics from St. John the Evangelist parish in Wellesley. In our pain, outrage, and sense of betrayal we came together six weeks ago to speak out about the crisis in our church. Strong feelings of anger, anguish, faith, and love of church moved us to put aside an hour after each mass on two consecutive weekends to address the pedophilia crisis.

Led by parish members, the listening sessions were a powerful indicator of the faithful's need to be heard individually and as Church, and of our need to speak out and to demand accountability and reform. Hundreds of parishioners participated in these sessions, and a weekly ninety-minute session has been initiated on Monday nights. Our number grows, and those from other parishes who need a place to have their voices heard have joined us. We call ourselves Voice of the Faithful.

Voice of the Faithful seeks consensus in order to effectively respond to this scandal threatening our church. We are sadly aware that pedophilia is a problem not only here but in other cities and countries. The culture of secrecy and abuses of power that produced this crisis must end. The overriding concerns that have emerged from our discussions are the desire to be fully responsive to the victims of pedophilia and their families, and to ensure that appropriate measures are taken to preclude future occurrences; to support clergy of integrity tarnished by this scandal; and to seek correction of the institutional structures of the Catholic Church that resulted in a gravely flawed response to this terrible betrayal of children.

We urge other parishes to consider this new model of Spirit-driven dialogue. Our weekly sessions are a model for consensus built on mutual respect, genuine listening, and a commitment to act. The Gospel of Jesus Christ demands our action in support of the most vulnerable among us. We expect archdiocesan leadership to hear us today and to provide channels for lasting communication and genuine collaboration.

Today, we raise our voices to claim our place at the table.

We are the Church. Come join us.

We are the Church. The words of Vatican II had seemed so revolutionary when we had first put them down on paper, and yet they were the words Father Tom had used. "You *are* the Church," he had told those attending our first meeting. And now we had listened as one of our own group stood and read our declaration with clarity and sincerity. It was a thrilling moment. It was also exciting to hear our stated expectation for the "archdiocesan leadership to hear us today and to provide channels for lasting communication and genuine collaboration." We wanted to come away from the day with something tangible—some specific process or format for communication and collaboration between laity and hierarchy.

As soon as Peggie finished we congratulated her and then the rest of us got up from our seats and stood in line, eager for a chance to add our own thoughts. It was a memorable moment: the women of our group lined up, ready to speak, a striking tableau of Pentecostal color at the Cardinal's convocation, proclaiming what we believed to be the truths of the day.

—◠—

At the front of the room, with his back to the chilly black waters of Boston Harbor, Bishop Lennon sat listening, occasionally nodding. Next to him was a recording secretary taking notes of what was said—later to be summarized and reported back to the plenary session.

A man from St. Joseph's parish in Needham moved to the microphone and proposed a nonbinding referendum at masses throughout the archdiocese on whether the Cardinal should resign. "The laity want to be heard," he said.

"The Cardinal has been a poor steward," said a woman who added that he was guilty of hubris.

There were, of course, some who were not critical of either the hierarchy or the Cardinal. A man from St. George's in Framingham stated that the ultimate child abuse was abortion. Another man urged people to stop paying attention to news coverage of the scandal. Prayer, he said, was the answer. Still another man said he was scandalized by a person who raised money for Catholic Charities and then spent weekends at an abortion clinic.

But such voices were in a distinct minority. A man from St. Paul's in Wellesley said he was concerned about the church losing members as a result of the scandal. He said he had heard that three Catholic families were recently introduced as new members of St. Andrew's Episcopal Church in Wellesley, having departed from Catholicism.

A confirmation teacher from Belmont was instructing a class of ninth graders on morality and asked, "What do we teach the children when they see a church that has hidden and protected evil?"

— I I I —

At the end of the session, dozens of people approached members of our group. Many asked for copies of our statement, others wondered how we had started. Some asked about the red dresses. Many asked whether they might come to our meetings.

Finally Maura returned from the Cardinal's session. She had not had the opportunity to read our statement—there were too many people ahead of her in line who wanted to speak. Cardinal Law had not heard our voice.

But Maura said that many people at the session had expressed sentiments similar to ours. We all wanted an end to the secrecy that had enabled the cover-up of sex abuse to occur. Though it was not unanimous, she said, there was a clear sense at the session that the Cardinal should resign.

A woman from St. Ignatius in Newton had told Cardinal

Law: "We need to change the whole power structure of the church. We need more women. The power, and the male dominance, and the secrecy are how this whole thing started."

The plenary session then began. The designated record keepers read off to the assemblage a summary of the points made at the various sessions. The summaries were accurate, brutally honest, and highly critical of the Cardinal, who sat listening.

Finally, Cardinal Law rose and spoke to us again. He said that he appreciated people expressing their honest concerns. He said he heard the expressions of "betrayal by the church, the archdiocese, and by me." He said, "I stand before you recognizing that the trust which many of you have had in me has been broken . . . because of decisions for which I was responsible, which I made. With all my heart, I am sorry for that, I apologize for that, and I will reflect on what this all means. You have my commitment . . . that I will do the best I can to find the course, the path, that will take us to where we need to be."

Speaking in a wistful tone, momentarily overcome with emotion, he asked, "Is there not the possibility that someone like me can bring us to where we need to go? I have heard you passionately and prayerfully plead for greater openness in the church . . . [and] I have heard calls for greater and more meaningful involvement of the laity in the life of the church, and specifically of women in the life of the church," he said. "I don't

have the answers today for all the things that I have heard. . . .
I have heard a great deal. And I need and I want . . . to really
take in what you have offered."

Svea felt like jumping to her feet and shouting, "But you
don't need to have all the answers because we want to help you."

He said that he would take what he had heard and he
would "ponder it."

And he was done.

That's it? Paul Baier wondered. Where were the channels of
communication for the laity? Where was the process by which
lay people could be involved in decision making? *That can't be
it.* Either he doesn't get it, Paul thought, or he's letting lawyers
think for him.

The convocation had been a defining moment for the Cardinal—and he had defined himself as aloof and unwilling to
reach out. He took an opportunity to mobilize a powerful force
of three thousand of the most active Catholics behind his leadership and instead gave many of us the incentive to build our
own organizations with which to help our church.

Mary Scanlon said what we all were thinking: "If he had
spoken from the heart and said, 'This is a terrible injustice, a terrible error in judgment I made. I want to open all the records of
past accusations and settlements concerning pedophilia by
priests.' If he had said, 'I'm going to move into a cabin and di-
vest the archdiocese of holdings to make restitution. I'm going
to end the culture of secrecy in the archdiocese, I'm going to en-

list the help of the laity.' If he had asked for the assistance of faithful people, we would have flocked to help him."

But that didn't happen.

—IV—

After the convocation I walked across the street to the Seaport Hotel, where organizers of the picketing had gathered. I saw Ann Barrett Doyle, a charismatic leader and tireless advocate for survivors. I suspected that her organizing skills and passion had helped generate the impressive demonstration outside the convocation. I told Ann and the others that I supported what they were doing, but that there were many Catholics who would never want to picket or protest. That's where I believed supporters for Voice of the Faithful would come from. I told them I thought protesting was a legitimate and effective form of expression that was needed. As a side effect, the protests permitted our group to be recognized as more moderate, more centrist than it might otherwise appear.

As our Wellesley group gathered to leave, we felt a great disappointment in the response of the Cardinal. But in addition to the disillusionment and anger at the hierarchy there was emerging a sense of empowerment as well. We left the convocation that day excited by the devotion, indignation, and intent of the laity to repair the damaged church.

"We did our job," said Paul Baier. "We came out of the hills and planted a flag of dissent in a faithful Catholic way. And there were three thousand other people saying they all felt the same way. We went away feeling we've got to do something about this."

The next morning, Sunday, March 10, the front-page headline in the *Globe* read: CATHOLIC LAY LEADERS URGE BROAD REFORMS. The story began, "In an extraordinary display of how the sexual abuse of children by priests has affected local Catholics, many of the church's top lay leaders yesterday told Cardinal Bernard F. Law that they want sweeping reforms of the church's structure."

The article quoted a woman from St. Ignatius parish in Newton. "In a strange way, this whole situation has really empowered Catholic people and priests at the parish level. I think we've kind of crossed a line, and I don't think we're going to go back."

Father Robert J. Bowers of St. Catherine of Siena in Charlestown said, "What came across is that this is a very articulate, well-educated, and deeply affected group of people who are going to say the truth. You're seeing loyalty at its very best. These people are going to love the church into something else, into a new birth."

The enormity of the mistake the Cardinal made by not embracing the laity and enlisting its help would soon be all too clear. It would subject him to harsh and unrelenting criticism even as it would fuel the growth of our organization.

CHAPTER 4

FINDING OUR PUBLIC VOICE

— I —

THE SCANDAL REVERBERATED throughout the world. While there were serious allegations of abuse in dozens of dioceses throughout the United States and around the world, there was no question that Boston was the epicenter of the crisis. Even President Bush got involved, speaking out in support of Cardinal Law. The president said the cardinal had contributed much to religious and civic life and added that he considered Cardinal Law "a man of integrity." He added, "I respect him a lot. I'm confident the church will clean up its business and do the right thing."

The hundreds who began to make a weekly pilgrimage to the basement of St. John's did not share the president's confidence. The growing crowds at our meetings reflected an outrage aimed at the church generally—from Boston to Rome—but that singled out Bernard Law as the embodiment of the scandal. Barely sixty days after the abuses first came to light, the *Boston Herald*, the more conservative of the two daily newspapers in Boston, called for the Cardinal to resign.

> Cardinal Law on several occasions has expressed
> sorrow and apologies for his handling of the affair
> and his tragic misjudgments. It is proper that he
> should do so, but sorrow does not make up for the
> sad fact that he has lost the trust of too many in his
> flock—some of them forever.

While it was not obvious to the general public, the editorial was of added significance because of the background of the publisher. Patrick Purcell was a Roman Catholic and had been a friend of the Cardinal. Purcell was also a parishioner at St. Julia's in Weston—the last parish in which John Geoghan had molested children. Geoghan had even performed the wedding ceremony for Purcell's daughter. Purcell told the *Globe* that the cardinal had "botched this thing terribly. He allowed Geoghan to be in a position to do harm to children. It's inexcusable. The more we see the evidence, the stream of people coming forward, the PR offensive, we had to say something." This from one of Bernard Law's friends and staunchest supporters, financially and otherwise.

Barely a week after the convocation, on March 19, another of the city's most influential businesspeople spoke out. David F. D'Alessandro, the chairman and chief executive officer of John Hancock Financial Services Inc., authored an op-ed article in the *Globe* in which he wrote that "there is only one way for the Archdiocese of Boston to put this scandal behind it and regain its rightful role as a force for good within our community. And that is with a new pastor and teacher and father at the top." D'Alessandro wrote that as CEO of Hancock he was ultimately in charge of the company's child-care center for employees. "If we had a pedophile who abused children here and I sent him off to treatment and then allowed him to go to work at another child-care center, I'd be arrested."

In such an environment it became clear to the archdiocesan administrators and fundraisers that their major annual event—the spring garden party at the Cardinal's residence, which in the past had raised millions—was in trouble. Contributions to the event had slumped. The few lay advisers who still had the Cardinal's confidence insisted that hosting an opulent event under such circumstances would be in the poorest of taste. The event was scrapped.

—◌◦◌—

After our brief public moment at the convocation, we returned to the basement of St. John's School determined to contribute our part so that the laity could work with the hierarchy and clergy to "do the right thing." But we had not yet agreed amongst ourselves what that should be.

We did recognize that we had to address the issue of our public visibility. First we had to decide whether we would accept the request of numerous reporters to attend our Monday night meetings. While some of us welcomed the coverage because it would spread the word, others were reluctant to open our meeting to the press, in part because of the second problem we were facing—we had yet to clearly define our mission. To many it seemed a little early to open our doors.

The debate about media presence had several aspects. Those opposed did not want to expose the deep emotional experiences that characterized our meetings. Voice of the Faithful had been born amidst an explosive mixture of heartbreak and rage. There was still a rawness to our emotion that made the prospect of a media presence feel somehow voyeuristic. Some of our members were wary that reporters would take our comments out of context and misinterpret what we were saying.

We knew that it would be difficult to convey the message that we were working against the scandal, and its causes, while remaining loyal to the Church. Martin Luther's protest was well known, but few knew that he wished to remain a member of the Church. We wanted to remain Catholic *and* have our voices heard. "It was scary enough to say what we were saying in church, much less to the press," observed Luise Dittrich.

As the discussion about whether to permit reporters to attend our meetings dragged on, a request for an interview came from one of the most trusted television newspeople in Boston. Natalie Jacobson had been prominent on Boston television for three decades. She was widely respected as an eminently decent person and straightforward journalist. In the wake of the convocation, she invited three members of Voice to come into her station, WCVB-TV, an ABC affiliate, for a discussion. This was different from allowing the media into our meetings; we saw it as an opportunity to extend our message to a wider audience. The group agreed that Peggie Thorp, Svea, and Jim Post would represent us in a televised discussion with Natalie, and the result was an excellent interview in which our representatives articulated our view of the scandal and our desire to do something about it.

With the interview having gone so well, and an offer by Channel 5 to set up a link to our Web site, the opposition to a media presence in our regular meetings decreased. Still there were reservations—enough so that there was real opposition to granting access to ABC News, which wanted to cover one of our meetings.

While the great majority of our members had become convinced that the benefits of media exposure outweighed the risks, a few remained adamantly opposed, and since from the beginning we operated on a principle of unanimity, we were forced to say no to ABC News.

I argued as strongly as I could that media coverage would advance our cause and was the best way not only to reach millions of other Catholics but also to capture the attention of the hierarchy. I had seen the powerful effect that accurate coverage from the media had had on our grassroots effort against nuclear weapons. While the members of International Physicians for the Prevention of Nuclear War had had similar arguments about the media, we had eventually welcomed reporters into all of our events. We would never have reached the millions essential to our task without media attention.

I likened the media to a spotlight that moved across the world covering topics of momentary interest. The spotlight was now directly on the Archdiocese of Boston, but it would soon move on and we might never again have such a chance. I argued that we would never be able to change the church by discussions restricted to St. John's basement; that if we waited until our mission statement was complete to open the meetings to the press—as some had argued—we would not even see it appear in the local Wellesley paper without paying for an ad. Because we were committed to the principle that we would not take major action without 100 percent agreement among our members, it would be a long time before we could agree on a mission statement.

"Why secrecy? What are we afraid of?" a young woman from Regis College asked pointedly, arguing that secrecy was clearly part of the problem with the church. Convinced by this argument, those opposed to the coverage agreed to accommodate the wish of the vast majority to open the meetings to the media. We began cautiously by inviting only the Wellesley cable TV station, the weekly town newspaper, and the *Boston Globe*, which had broken the story.

And so the dam burst. Once our decision was made we were inundated with media coverage—reporters from major American newspapers and magazines, from the television networks, from Ireland, England, Denmark, Italy, and elsewhere.

While our initial deliberations over media access showed a certain naïveté and had cost us some initial exposure, it did reveal a purity of motive within the group and, in the long run, probably increased the media coverage.

— I I —

As we continued our Monday night meetings, which now had about two hundred attendees, we knew we needed to agree on a common path of action. Although Voice was only six weeks old, the time had come to define our general mission and specific goals in writing. Fortunately, the need to write a consensus declaration for the Cardinal's convocation had provided a start, but the declaration was not quite sharp enough. Also, we now had many new members who had not participated in its preparation. Thus, during our regular Monday night meetings we began drafting a mission statement.

Newcomers and veterans were in complete agreement that our first goal was to be responsive to survivors. The second goal, which we had enunciated in our convocation statement, was also obvious: to support clergy of integrity. Most of us in Voice had been blessed with fulfilling relationships with priests through the years and we wanted to demonstrate our emphatic and ongoing support for these fine men.

Our third goal arose from a desire to address the underlying cause of scandal. We wanted to ensure that never again would there be a scandal of this magnitude; never again would priests be permitted to abuse children, never again would there be a deliberate cover-up by hierarchy of such evil and illegal behavior. We also knew that the Church had other severe problems, known prior to this scandal, which we intended to address. These included issues such as the precipitous decline in the number of young men joining the priesthood, the decrease in weekly attendance at mass, the questions over the role of women in the Church, and the lack of interest of many young people in Catholicism. Our list of issues included these and was similar to that which Cardinal Joseph Bernardin had proposed for discussion in 1996 in his Common Ground initiative. We knew that the laity needed a mechanism to identify its own views on these issues, many of which could lead to structural change in the administration of the Church.

We had examined the most commonly offered explanations of what had led to the sexual abuse and cover-up: a lack of married and female priests, homosexuality, and too much, or too little, of Vatican II. But we sensed that these features of the church were not the primary problem. After intense and prolonged discussions, we concluded that the underlying cause of the *institutional* failure of the Church—the cover-up—was the excessive power of the hierarchy resulting from the absence of a meaningful voice of the laity.

Finally, after continued discussion and with the help of a PowerPoint presentation illustrating the present structure of the Church, the group decided that our third goal would be: "To shape structural change within the church." The structural change we were seeking would allow for a more participatory decision-making process, the opening of records, and letting light shine in upon the assignment, transfer, and personnel records of priests. It would mean changing the way that the church conducts its business—changing structure, not doctrine. It would address what we believed to be the underlying cause of the scandal—the concentration of power and secrecy that were part of the culture of the hierarchy. It would, in short, provide a meaningful place at the table where the voice of the laity could be heard.

With our newly clarified goals in mind, and after extensive debate, we settled upon a concise mission statement: "To provide a prayerful voice, attentive to the Spirit, through which the Faithful can actively participate in the governance and guidance of the Catholic Church."

Voice of the Faithful was now like a small mustard seed that had fallen on fertile ground. Its rapid development was being fostered by a deluge of new stories of abuse, cover-up, and arrogant responses from the hierarchy. Pressure on Cardinal Law increased as he continued to respond to criticism with condescension. Outrage, within the Catholic community of Boston and beyond, continued to grow.

— III —

At this critical juncture, Paul Baier, one of our youngest members at the time, hatched a bold plan to spread the spirit of Voice beyond St. John's and Boston—a plan that Paul of the Gospel, who had spread the teachings of Christ to the Corinthians, Ephesians, and beyond, or the Paul Revere of Boston, would surely have endorsed. Our Paul knew that in the months ahead the intense media coverage of the scandal would wane, and it would then be difficult, if not impossible, to spread the important ideas for lay activism that were being developed at St. John's.

And so on the evening of Monday, March 18, Paul stood up and stepped into the open circle that still formed the center of our meetings. What he said stunned the group. He urged that Voice—a six-week-old unincorporated discussion group, with no officers, no official members, no insurance, and extremely limited funds—hold a national convention within four months, with the goal of attracting Catholics from throughout the United States and the rest of the world.

After a pause, the group began to respond. People thought the idea brilliant or crazy or both. Our biggest external action to date had been coordinating a dozen people to agree upon a one-page statement and present it at the Cardinal's convocation. Convening a national meeting of Catholics with a small, all-volunteer organization committed to consensus decision making seemed well beyond our reach.

While most of us had remained focused on our group's activities in and around Boston, Paul had been receiving signs that our message was already resonating in the larger world. One of his activities since the beginning of Voice had been to send a weekly e-mail update to anyone who had signed up on our Web site and I had urged him to add his name to this update so that those who were just becoming aware of Voice could identify with an individual. He added his personal spiritual reflections to these factual updates, and thousands of concerned Catholics from throughout the world began to look forward to their weekly letter from Paul. This rapidly growing online community also began sending Paul dozens of e-mails each week in response. Many told of the hope that Voice brought to them in a time of darkness for the church. Paul saw the convention as a way to build on this sense of hope and community. Paul wanted to reach out to the millions of active as well as disaffected Catholics and let them know that they need not despair; that they could join a fight to save the church.

"The convention would be a pivotal event," Paul argued. "It would re-energize press coverage and send a message to the bishops that the laity—who represent 99 percent of the members of the church, and 99 percent of the donations—are not going to sit idly by and watch this crisis."

Initially, though, we were paralyzed by the proposal. Our inherently cautious group clearly saw the downside. If our fledgling organization took on this task and failed—if the media were to show up and find a half-empty hall—our credibility would be severely damaged.

After the meeting, a number of our most active members approached Paul to express their concerns. Scott Fraser, Svea's husband, a consultant at a major accounting firm and our treasurer, spoke frankly to Paul. The convention would cost in excess of $100,000, Scott said, quoting Paul's estimate, and yet the group had barely $5,000—which we had raised by passing the hat each week—in the bank.

Paul was undeterred. He believed the convention would succeed. As an entrepreneur he had seen crazy sales deals and long-shot investments become reality in a very short period of time. Paul persuaded the group to grant him the authority to at least explore the possibility—to see whether a host facility might be available and what the cost would be.

The next morning, with the clock ticking, Paul started working the phone. He learned that there were only three places in Boston able to handle a convention of this magnitude, and of these only the Hynes Convention Center Auditorium was available on a Saturday during the summer. The date was July 20; the price was $10,000.

The woman he spoke with at the Convention Center then asked whether we had insurance, which we did not, and that was a deal breaker—no insurance, no convention. Paul had a decision to make. He could take the information back to the group and engage in debate over whether to proceed. He knew the debate would be prolonged, and possibly lead to a decision not to have the convention. He asked the woman what it could cost to hold the space. She said $1,000 and insurance.

Paul phoned a friend who had sold him insurance in his dot.com ventures, who faxed a coverage sheet within hours. Paul then wrote a personal check for a thousand dollars to hold all 4,200 seats.

At our April 8 meeting, Paul returned to the center of our open circle, which now included more than three hundred people. He told the group that he had temporarily secured space for a national Voice convention. Without asking for discussion as to whether or not we should proceed, he issued an amazing announcement: He would personally donate the full $10,000 needed to pay for the rental of Hynes Auditorium and the necessary insurance.

After a stunned moment of silence, the room burst into applause. Paul had led Voice to a bold decision—it would host a national convention.

— I V —

Meanwhile, as the New England winter turned to spring, the scandal intensified. Every time we concluded that it could not possibly get worse, a new atrocity surfaced. On the morning of April 7, for example, the *Globe* reported a page-one story under the headline "CALIFORNIA PARISH SAYS BOSTON KEPT QUIET ON ACCUSED PRIEST." The lead paragraph stated: "Despite three decades of complaints that the Rev. Paul R. Shanley had sexually abused children, the Boston Archdiocese transferred the onetime 'street priest' to a California parish where officials were never told of the molestation allegations." The article went on to say:

> Shanley's alleged victims in the Archdiocese of
> Boston included a 42-year-old South Shore man
> who received a $40,000 settlement from the arch-
> diocese in 1991 after notifying church officials that

he had repeatedly been anally raped by Shanley in about 1972, when he was 12 or 13.

The alleged victim, who asked that his name not be used, said he met Shanley after responding to a newspaper advertisement the priest had placed encouraging troubled teenagers to contact him for counseling.

This news fueled a renewed surge of anger and increased attendance at our next Monday night meeting. More than four hundred people showed up—the most ever. During the meeting I emphasized that in spite of the intense anger people felt at Cardinal Law, it was critically important that Voice continue to focus on the flawed structure of the church rather than on the mistakes of a single leader. We also briefly discussed the hot-button issues of celibacy, women priests, homosexuality, and other redundant topics that many felt contributed to the sexual abuse. I hoped we could set these controversial topics aside because I knew the laity was split on these issues and, as I learned in my work with the antinuclear movement, building consensus was key to our success.

In the early 1980s, many liberals spoke against the acceleration of the nuclear arms race, but it continued without a pause. As physicians, we sought to convince both liberals and conservatives that a nuclear war *could not be won*. To do this we presented medical facts and sought conservative allies. I spoke with the leaders of the American Legion, and eventually obtained a letter from President Reagan supporting our work. My father helped enlist the American Medical Association to support International Physicians for the Prevention of Nuclear War. In fact, the Nobel Prize committee recognized the centrist nature of our work in its citation. To change the church we would need to construct an organization that would be considered useful and acceptable to moderate Catholics and yet still engage a sizable number of those on either extreme, who are the most likely to devote time and energy to the organization because of the strength of their views. Liberals, by definition, wanted change in the church, and Voice was a movement for fundamental change—thus liberals were easily engaged. Moderates, who generally would not be involved in church politics, were driven to action by the scandal. Special efforts, however, were needed to convince conservatives that Voice was not simply a vehicle created by the left to promote a predetermined agenda.

From the beginning, Voice of the Faithful was blessed with a group of conservative Catholics who had the courage and conviction to speak out in our formative meetings, despite their minority status. Debra Tomazewski had been close to Cardinal Law and spoke passionately on his behalf. Her twin sister, Ann Urban, shared Debra's traditional views, yet contributed her organizational skills to the group as coordinator of our meetings. Richard Crino, a mainstay of the St. John's choir, brought his traditional views and business strategy to our meetings. David Castaldi, a devout Catholic from Notre Dame, had, after a successful career in business, served as the chancellor of the archdiocese, the highest position for a lay leader. His experience and personal friendship with many members of the hierarchy helped Voice pursue a path that sought partnership rather than confrontation.

The majority of my own views had been nurtured in the liberal and social-activist spirit of Vatican II. In addition to my many years in the international peace movement, I also founded a group to represent students at the Johns Hopkins School of Medicine, a neighborhood association in Newton, and an organization working for increased federal funding for medical research. Peggie Thorp's view was that our most active members were products of sixties-style activism. She told a reporter from the *Los Angeles Times*, "Our age group was defined by movements, for peace, racial justice, women's rights." Peggie felt a powerful impulse toward democratization and believed that just as there was a Conference of Bishops and a College of Cardinals, there would one day be a Conference of the Laity—with an equal voice on matters other than the core doctrine of the faith.

— V —

While the steady stream of revelations continued across the country, in Boston the Shanley case continued to draw particular attention. The *Globe* reported on April 9 that "For more than a decade, Cardinal Bernard F. Law and his deputies ignored allegations of sexual misconduct against Rev. Paul R. Shanley and reacted casually to complaints that Shanley endorsed sexual relations between men and boys, according to an avalanche of documents that were made public yesterday."

The Shanley documents revealed that Cardinal Law had knowingly and on numerous occasions enabled Shanley to hold positions in which he could engage in activities with children. Documents revealed that Law praised Shanley for "years of generous and zealous care" and an "impressive record."

Eric MacLeish, a Boston lawyer working for numerous victims of sexual abuse by clergy, stated that one of his clients, Gregory Ford, had been taken out of a catechism class at age six and raped by Shanley. The Shanley files included the revelation that Shanley had attended meetings of a group that would become the North American Man Boy Love Association (NAMBLA), which openly advocated sex between men and boys.

These revelations brought a firestorm down upon Cardinal Law and a new chorus calling for his resignation, including an editorial in the *Globe*. Jack Connors, a prominent Boston civic leader who had earlier expressed his concern over the actions of the Cardinal, now said he should go. A sixty-five-year-old woman was quoted in the newspaper as saying she had been an ardent supporter of the Cardinal but that these revelations made her want "to vomit."

A few days after the Shanley revelations, Cardinal Law announced that he would remain as Archbishop of Boston. There was also a rumor that he had actually offered his resignation to the Pope but that it had been rejected.

The latest scandal increased the pressure on Voice, from both inside and outside the group, to take a stand on whether Cardinal Law should resign. I had tried to avoid the debate because I suspected it would be divisive, and I never believed the behavior of the Cardinal was as important as the underlying problem of the unbalanced power of the office. I was also concerned that a call for his resignation would put us in direct conflict with the hierarchy, thus diminishing our appeal to centrists and conservatives.

Nevertheless, the new horror of the Shanley case forced the issue upon us. The night after the Cardinal announced that he would remain as leader of the Archdiocese of Boston, the moment had arrived for Voice to take a stand.

— V I —

The April evening was chilly and damp, but St. John's School parking lot was alive with television trucks and a bustling crowd. I stepped up on the small two-foot stage—a stage on which my daughter had performed in various church recitals as a first-grader. While our PowerPoint projector was being readied, I looked out at hundreds of faces angered and anguished by the latest Shanley revelations. It wasn't blood they wanted, exactly—it wasn't vengeance. But I knew that these good people wanted a chance to express their moral outrage against the cover-up by Cardinal Law.

To my right was a bank of five television cameras, ready to transmit the event to millions. Many people were attending their first meeting. Some had traveled from as far away as western Massachusetts, New Hampshire, and even Buffalo, New York.

We began the session, as we always did, with a prayer, followed by an invitation for those new to the group to speak if they wished to do so. This was a crucial element of our meetings because it brought us back to our beginnings—it re-created the power of our early meetings when members of a small group had sat listening to one another. A woman from West Roxbury said she considered the formation of Voice to be a "watershed event. My whole life I've been dreaming about this meeting." Another woman wondered aloud whether it might be possible some day for her grandniece to become a cardinal.

And then it was time for our decision regarding a call for the Cardinal's resignation. I knew from similar consensus discussions in the peace movement that it was important to agree on the rules before we got into a debate and battle lines hardened. I reviewed our policy, adhered to since the beginning of the group, that all major actions required unanimous approval. Consensus had helped us make centrist decisions, and when we did choose to act, we did so with a cohesive sense of unanimity. No one was left behind. I was unsure how it would serve us in this charged setting with more than three hundred participants.

I made it clear that in order for Voice *as an organization* to call for the Cardinal's resignation, a unanimous vote would be required. Did that mean everyone had to favor every word of our proposed statement? No, I told the group, but it did mean that everybody had to be willing to tolerate it. "You don't have to like it, but everyone must be willing to go forward with it." I then read to the group the statement, projected on Power-Point, which the steering committee, under Jim Post's leadership, had drafted:

The Possible Resignation of Cardinal Law

Whereas Cardinal Bernard F. Law has lost the confidence of the faithful in his administration and leadership of the Archdiocese of Boston, we believe that a change in leadership is essential.

We therefore call upon the Cardinal to step down as Archbishop of Boston.

We make this request because Cardinal Law has indicated his intention to remain in his position. We are aware that a news report states that Cardinal Law has already offered his resignation, but that it was rejected by the Vatican. If this is the case, we believe that such a decision reflects a lack of understanding by the Vatican of the situation in Boston, and call upon the Vatican leaders responsible for the decision to meet with a delegation of laity from Boston who can provide a full report on the local situation.

When the resignation issue is resolved, we call upon the Vatican to support the people of Boston by engaging in a process of consultation with the laity to determine his successor.

I introduced Jim Post and said that I hoped the group would approve the statement so that we could send it to Rome in time for the meeting the following week of Catholic bishops with the Pope.

The intense feelings of those in the audience led to a barrage of passionate statements. One individual stated that the Cardinal had lost his moral authority to govern by his cover-up of the crimes of Shanley, Geoghan, and others, and that he was guilty of criminal offenses. A woman whose son had been abused by a priest recalled the horror that her child had experienced and pleaded with us to vote for resignation. The pain and emotion of her plea overwhelmed her, and in the heat of the moment she fell faint to one side, caught and ministered to by members of the group. The outrage of each speaker was exceeded by the next as the temperature in the room rose and these fervent Catholics, many of whom had never uttered a dissenting word in their lives, demanded that their cardinal resign.

But not everyone argued for resignation. One man said that when his family had faced a particularly difficult time, Cardinal Law had counseled them and helped them through it. The man said he could never forget that and could never fail to respect what Law had done, as a priest and a person. Another said, "The problem is not the Cardinal but goes beyond the Cardinal to the culture of the church." He added, "The Cardinal is not the ogre the press makes him out to be." Someone else said that we as Catholics should find it in our hearts to forgive. Another said that the Cardinal had once helped him with his job and he wanted to return the favor by not calling for his resignation.

There were angry denunciations on both sides. "He should stay and expiate by undoing all the evil he's done!" someone shouted. Someone else cried out, "He's a criminal and a disgrace. He must resign!" Someone said that we were not ready to call for his resignation, to which another shouted a reply: "We should have called for his resignation weeks ago!"

Scott and Svea Fraser were standing off to the side, near the wall. Svea had been rocked by a sense of betrayal, yet she was uncertain what to do. Svea had a deep and abiding belief in the power of forgiveness. As she listened to the debate raging around her, Svea felt torn. She felt as though the group should make some sort of statement about how irresponsible Law had been, yet she wasn't sure that she should vote for his resignation. Calling for the resignation of a cardinal seemed to her a drastic move. When Scott finally spoke up and said, "Christians must make decisions with compassion and forgiveness," his statement was met with roiling anger.

Debra Tomazewski stood to speak in support of Law, saying that he should be given a chance to correct his mistakes. At least five people immediately began shouting at her, preventing her from completing her comments. I used the power of the microphone and the chair to insist that the shouting stop and that Debra be heard.

Mary Scanlon listened to Debra's argument but couldn't agree. She thought that the one who is wronged has the power to grant forgiveness—and the survivors had not forgiven Cardinal Law. Mary felt strongly that it was necessary for the Cardinal to reconcile first with those who had been wronged, and that no one else should be empowered to offer forgiveness until that occurred.

Paul Baier considered the Cardinal increasingly culpable in light of the Shanley revelations. He also viewed the Cardinal as an incompetent crisis manager. He believed that the combination of his incompetence and intransigence was clearly hurting the moral authority of the church.

By the time I called for a vote, it was clear from the discussion that the overwhelming majority of those present wanted the Cardinal to resign. When I asked those in favor of resignation to stand, 90-plus percent quickly rose to their feet. I then called for those opposed to stand, not knowing if those who had expressed opposition would abstain. About ten brave individuals stood. I announced that the resolution as written had not passed, and, as things stood, we would not be calling for the Cardinal's resignation.

My statement was greeted with shouts from dozens of angry participants. I saw a number of people leaving the meeting, shouting and shaking their heads in disgust. I asked each of the dissenters, who remained standing, if they could explain their reasons for opposition, in the hopes that we could redraft the document in a manner they could accept. Jim Post and I both offered wording changes to the resolution in an effort to make it palatable to the dissenters, but this only led to another cycle of accusations and shouting with no sign of resolution. People grew even angrier and threw up their hands, some shouting at me as they left.

We had been engaged in exhausting debate for almost two hours. Terry McKiernan, one of the first people from outside St. John's to join our group, thought it was madness that we let anyone who walked in off the street hold veto power over the entire organization. Although I had served before as moderator of many contentious discussions in my medical research work and with social causes, I had never seen such a loss of control of a meeting, even as a participant, much less as moderator. I stood helplessly on the stage as the arguing continued among the diehards who remained.

And then Maura O'Brien, a lawyer and former member of the Wellesley town government, whispered a suggestion in my ear. She said that Ginny Murray, who was also experienced with town meetings, had suggested calling for a nonbinding "sense of the meeting" vote. I explained to the group that this would allow us to express an overwhelming sense that people favored the document that called for Cardinal Law to resign. But because of the ground rules, the document would not become Voice policy.

Miraculously, this proposal appealed to all combatants, and a "sense of the meeting" vote was taken. The result was 219 in favor of resignation, and 9 opposed, with 5 abstentions. Those favoring resignation felt the majority view was expressed, while those opposed felt their opposition had been heard.

When the vote had been completed "there was no sense of joy or glee," said Svea. "It was very painful for all of us. People were in tears over it."

On the other hand, Svea felt gratified that the group had expressed its anguish and betrayal, and that we had stayed together as a movement. Her stomach was tied in knots, yet she also felt that the "sense of the meeting" vote had been liberating, allowing her to register her strong concerns without the vote actually being a call by the organization to remove the Cardinal from office. She felt that the Spirit had guided the deliberations and helped us produce the right result.

I left the meeting exhausted and discouraged. I was distressed by my inability to manage the tumult, and appreciative of Maura and Ginny for their suggestion that rescued us from complete disaster. I felt we had lost many supporters who concluded that Voice was too disorganized, cautious, or ineffectual for its ambitious goal of changing the church. I was convinced that at this stage of our growth we should abandon the unanimity rule in favor of a two-thirds-majority vote for major policy issues. It would be an easy sell. Even those who feared they might be in the minority needed no more graphic demonstration that we had outgrown the requirement for 100 percent agreement than the debacle they had just witnessed.

It was apparent that once we changed to a two-thirds rule, it would be easy to vote for Cardinal Law's resignation. But to honor the process we had followed, we could not bring up the resignation question for another vote until considerable time had passed.

As the days went by, I thought of the resignation debate as an evening of excruciating birth pains for the group. And I began to think that the result of the debate—our decision, as an organization, not to call for the resignation of the Cardinal—was a blessing for Voice. By *not* calling for Law to resign, we helped others perceive us as the moderate group we actually were—an understanding that was absolutely essential for success. We also sent a message to the hierarchy and our fellow Catholics that we did not consider the scandal to be a failure of one person, in one city, at one moment. Rather, it fit with our focus on the broader issue of structural change. Perhaps the Holy Spirit *had* actually run the meeting. I know I certainly hadn't.

CHAPTER 5

A GROWING PRAYERFUL VOICE SPEAKS TO SURVIVORS

— I —

FORTUNATELY, THE CARDINAL LAW controversy and our sometimes heated battles were not all that occupied Voice of the Faithful during the spring of 2002. While many of us were consumed with these essential tasks, another group of Voice activists was hard at work on what we called Prayerful Voice. Under the skilled leadership of Susan Troy, with her master's of divinity degree, the group was developing the spiritual core of Voice of the Faithful, including creating prayers to address the crisis. We also had a Survivors Group in which Mary Scanlon, Jeanette Post, and Andrea Johnson brought their professional experience in the healing professions to bear toward our goal of supporting the survivors. The members of Voice of the Faithful Survivors Working Group were reaching out and listening to survivors and devising ways we could actively support them. Working groups have always been an essential element of Voice. From day one we had been a collaborative organization—our insistence on unanimity when making decisions had been the clearest example of that—and the working groups were all about collaboration. Such a cooperative effort between our working groups on prayer and survivors was about to produce one of our most moving events.

While many positive encounters had occurred privately between Voice members and survivors, Voice had received some criticism in this area. Some survivors who favored a more forceful protest against the Cardinal thought we should join the survivors in their protests held in front of the Cardinal's residence and the Cathedral of the Holy Cross in Boston's South End. While some in Voice favored participation in these protests, the organization as a whole held a more moderate view, reflecting our determination to stay centrist.

But there was more to it than that. Some survivors had come forward with their stories many years earlier and we, the Catholic laity, had not responded. In some cases we attacked them for revealing the terrible truth.

Finally, in a criticism that cut deeply into the soul of Voice, we were said to be opportunists using the crimes against survivors to advance a separate agenda to change the church. "You will get your women priests by climbing on the backs of the survivors," it was said. The criticism hurt because while we did not advocate women's ordination, we did have a goal of church reform that went beyond the immediate concerns of many survivors. My fear was that the hierarchy would succeed in quieting the sexual abuse issue without addressing the underlying cause, as had been done in Dallas a decade earlier, when a sexual abuse scandal had been dealt with on the surface and quickly forgotten.

I felt that our work for church reform could be defended as a direct response to the abuse the survivors had experienced. On an individual level, they had been abused by individual priests with the power of adulthood and a Roman collar. They were further abused by the collective force of the hierarchy, who covered up the crimes and even now refused to atone for the damage. Voice was not seeking women priests or any specific goal of church reform. We sought to address the imbalance of power that made the scandal possible. With the laity involved in the decision making of the church—with mothers and fathers playing an active role—the sex abuse scandal would never have happened. It could happen only in a culture of single males who believed that they were superior to their flock; who believed covering up crimes by priests to protect the reputation of the church was more important than protecting children.

We passionately wanted to strengthen our relationship with survivors, to show them we cared. And Susan Troy, and her colleague Lynn Finn, came up with the ideal way for us to do it— a healing mass in which the laity, with the help of Voice, could begin the reconciliation between the church and the survivors that the hierarchy had failed to initiate.

"We knew that success for Voice was possible only if we continued to ground ourselves in faith and prayer," said Susan Troy. Susan created the liturgy for the healing mass along with other members of Prayerful Voice as well as Father Tom Powers and Sister Evelyn Ronan, S.N.D. Sister Evelyn was a particularly important presence in our parish. She was a religious sister who had held a major position at the chancery and now served as Pastoral Associate at St. John's. She was a kind of guardian angel of our movement.

We were blessed to have Susan Troy's inspirational leadership for this mass. Susan is a mother of three children ranging in age from 19 to 24 and had always been a spiritual person. She received her undergraduate degree from Trinity College in Washington and her master's in speech and drama from Catholic University. She went on to work in the labor movement promoting the advancement of women in the construction field and other nontraditional work places. In 1989, when her family moved to Wellesley and joined St. John's, Susan immediately became active. She led the family liturgy program, which attracted standing-room-only crowds. She worked in religious education and preparation of children for the sacraments.

In the early 1990s, she "felt called forth" to seek a higher degree. She was accepted into the master's in divinity program at the Weston Jesuit School of Theology in Cambridge, Massachusetts. She went through the four-year program in a class of about sixty-five, mostly Jesuits, but about thirty percent of the class were women. Many of her female classmates "entered as Catholics and left as something else," said Susan. "They left the church and were ordained in other churches."

"We shared the campus with the Episcopal Divinity School and many of the Episcopal women were on an ordination track—an option that was not open to the Catholic women."

With her training completed in 1998, Susan was more committed than ever to her work within the church. She headed Prayerful Voice and channeled her considerable energy into the healing mass.

On Friday evening, April 26, a chilly spring night, more than seven hundred people gathered at St. John's. The mood was solemn and spirit-filled as the faithful from all over the Greater Boston area gathered to celebrate a Eucharist for those who had suffered so much at the hands of the church. Voice members, standing at the doors of the church, offered to apply ashes to peoples' foreheads as a visible sign of penance. From the lectern, Susan Troy offered a greeting and explanation at the beginning of mass.

"Welcome to this prayerful moment, to this Mass of Healing in response to the crisis of abuse and betrayal in our Church. I am Susan Troy, a member of St. John's parish and of Voice of the Faithful. We are new friends and companions on a difficult journey. It is good to be *together*."

Susan announced that our mass would be concelebrated by Father Tom, our former pastor Monsignor John Philbin, and a third priest, Father Bill Kremmel, who was in residence at St. John's and chaplain at Regis and Framingham state colleges.

Susan read:

We have gathered in silence, signed with ashes, symbolic of our sorrow and the shame those abused have been forced to carry too long.

This is already an amazing and powerful gathering of the Spirit. Our need is for a space for being together in prayer: victims, survivors, and all those who long to support them and to heal the brokenness in our Church.

Emotions are deep and feelings need to be expressed. This evening of gathering, prayer and Eucharist is to be a sacred space for all of us to bring our strongest feelings. It is a place where we hope peace can begin for each of us.

Father Tom Powers said that we are "painfully aware of the sinful nature of our community and we beg for God's forgiveness. . . . We ask for forgiveness for those in leadership in our church who have failed to use their position of trust and authority to ensure the safety of our children. Give them courage and wisdom to assume responsibility for their misguided actions . . ."

Then came a reading from the Book of Lamentations by Sister Evelyn: "I have forgotten what happiness is . . . let not your ear be deaf to my cry for help." It seemed strikingly appropriate for the occasion.

A reading from the First Letter of St. Paul to the Corinthians (12:12–26) spoke of the unity we all sought:

> As a body is one, though it has many parts, and all
> the parts of the body, though many, are one body,
> so also Christ. . . . Now the body is not a single
> part, but many. . . . [T]he parts of the body that
> seem to be weaker are all the more necessary, and
> those parts of the body that we consider less honor-
> able we surround with greater honor, and our less
> presentable parts are treated with greater propriety,
> whereas our more presentable parts do not need
> this. But God has so constructed the body as to give
> greater honor to a part that is without it, so that

there may be no division in the body, but that the parts have the same concern for one another. If one part suffers, all the parts suffer with it; if one part is honored, all the parts share its joy.

Susan Troy and others then led us in the prayer of the faithful which had been written by Susan specifically for this special mass:

> *For all those who were abused by clergy, we embrace you; we pray that as the people of God we can in some real way be agents of your healing. We are over-whelmed by the knowledge of your pain and suffering; you are precious in God's sight. May you feel God's healing love in every way and in everything. We pray to the Lord.*

We responded: "Lord, hear our prayer." Susan read:

> *For all the families of those who have been abused. For the pain and suffering you have endured, we pray for healing and new life. For all that was not heard, for the pleas that went unanswered, for the pain and be-trayal that was not shared, we pray for forgiveness. We pray to the Lord. . . .*
>
> *For all those who have experienced sexual, phys-*

ical, and emotional abuse and degradation, we ac-knowledge your pain and suffering and cry out against such sinfulness. For all those marginalized by abuses of power and by hatred, we ask for healing and whole-ness. We pray to the Lord. . . .

For the faithful who have been betrayed by those we trusted, by those who are said to lead us in the name of Jesus Christ, we pray for an increase of faith, for the holy wisdom to understand and accept espe-cially in this Easter season that sin and death are not the final answers, but that we are called each day to new life. We pray to the Lord. . . .

For the failure of the Catholic Church to be a true sign of the power of God's unconditional love and need for each of us, and for all those who have been unable to remain in full communion with our Church, we pray for the growth in holiness, which will welcome you all home. We pray to the Lord. . . .

For priests of integrity and all women religious who toil in the vineyard and endure their own sense of betrayal and abandonment, we pray that the voice of the faithful will be a witness to you of Jesus' love and communion with you and that you know the voice of the faithful is raised in Thanksgiving for your voca-tion. We pray to the Lord. . . .

For our Church, that it remains truly

grounded in the Gospel of Jesus Christ, a commu-
nion of believers, transfigured by the good news of
Jesus Christ, who together do the work of building
up the Reign of God in our hearts and in our
world. . . .

For our church leaders, that they be renewed by
the action of the Holy Spirit in their midst. May
they welcome the spiritual gifts of humility, wisdom,
and courage; may the image of Jesus as Good Shep-
herd, listening, guarding, and caring, inform all
they do in the name of God. We pray to the
Lord . . .

As Father Tom stood in front of the altar and prepared to speak, a solemn hush settled upon our congregation. The reading from the Book of Luke was the story of Jesus teaching in a synagogue on the Sabbath where he had healed a crippled woman, and Jesus had been sharply criticized by the leader of the synagogue for curing the woman on the Sabbath.

Father Tom summoned the image of the woman "bent down, bent down for so long. She is an image of our faith community bent down . . . weighted down by the crisis, the sins, the scandal that we are now coping with."

He continued. "This woman is invited to stand up and be healed by God's love, and that the invitation from Jesus has been extended to all of us." He said that there was a painful time when we had searched to find what had gone wrong with our church, but that now we were gradually beginning to stand up.

"There is pain and suffering for victims and survivors for which there are no words," Father Tom concluded. "There are no words . . ." And because there were no words, he invited us to join him in a moment of silence.

And so we fell silent. But it was not one of those moments of silence that seem pro forma, that last all of ten seconds. This was a moment of profound silence and reflection—three solid minutes during which the silence was such that there could be heard no sound, no movement, no disturbance of any kind. There was an incredible sense of God's presence, the Spirit with us, in our midst. I discovered many others had a similar feeling—and the mass continues to be talked about to this day as a defining moment for Voice.

Father Tom then said that the bent woman "stood up straight and let God's glory touch her face. With the support of one another, let us stand up and let God's glory touch our face."

And we did.

— I I —

In keeping with the prayerful intent of the mass, Susan announced that the proceeds of the collection would go to benefit Survivors Network of those Abused by Priests (SNAP), an organization of survivors who had been working to help victims of priest sex abuse since 1991.

When time came for distribution of the Holy Communion, more than twenty lay people who served as Eucharistic Ministers crowded together on the altar with our three priests. This scene, for Susan Troy, was "a visible symbol. All these men and women who were eucharistic ministers—such a symbol of the transforming power of what was going on with Voice."

When communion was over, we prayed again:

You are not alone anymore. We, those present and those unable to be here, want to journey with you through your pain and anger. We are listening to your pain, and we are hearing you. We wish for you an end to this long period of sorrow. We pray that your journey be filled with a new awareness of the care and tenderness with which we hold you in our hearts. Most of all, we pray for your healing and the freedom that the grace of forgiveness brings. On this night, we lift you to God for all that God longs to give to you—and in all time to come, we will continue to do so.

In the congregation there was an older woman who broke into sobs. She appeared to have come alone, and yet she was comforted by those around her. "My child was abused and I haven't been to mass in twenty-five years," she said through tears.

Tim and Julie Dempsey, too, said they felt a sense of comfort they had never experienced in the two decades since their son had been molested by a priest. They had come from St. Mary's in Lynn, where Tim was a deacon. The archdiocese had initially paid for counseling for their son but then abruptly cut it off after just six months. Cardinal Law himself met with the family and provided an assurance that payment would be forthcoming to help the family. But there was nothing.

The healing mass was a defining moment; a moment that brought a unique sense of comfort to Tim and Julie. "It was the first time we heard those words of comfort," Tim said. "The first time we heard, 'I am sorry for what you are feeling, sorry we did not speak up earlier, I am sorry and we embrace you.' It touched me very personally."

This spiritual journey did not end in the church. After the celebration of the liturgy was completed, Susan Troy asked the congregation to light candles and walk in procession out of the front doors and to gather in front of the church. This would be for those present, she said, "a sign of our movement from sorrow to light . . . spread light throughout this congregation, the light of Christ that we carry into the world."

Silently, with a collective solemnity that comes easily to a group of individuals steeped in the Catholic tradition, the congregation filed down the ten broad steps at the front of the church into the darkness of a cool spring evening, holding the candles they had been given. Soon, a magnificent circle of light, brought by the faithful in collective worship of the Lord, surrounded St. John's.

The glow from the mass of candles spread out into the night to the world beyond. Traffic on Washington Street slowed as those in passing cars could not help but take note of the event. I looked over at Susan Troy and thought how much richer the Catholic Church would be if it made it easier for women like Susan to more effectively contribute their great talents to a needy church. This healing mass—in sharp contrast to the mass experienced at the Cardinal's convocation—had a gentle, receptive, loving feel.

Svea looked around at everyone holding their candles. She saw that the moon hung in the night sky, and noted that everyone stood quite still. She felt a deep sense of unity, a sense that we were all joined in common purpose. In this service dedicated to the survivors and to the healing of our church, we were united in a visible sign, an acknowledgment of the truth of the horrible things that had happened. We were now present for the victims, for the survivors, as we had not been before.

I thought about the work ahead, and the need to permit the truth of the moment to spread throughout the world. I felt the glow of our candles symbolize the light of Christ going out to the world, as the message of the Voice of the Faithful had started to do. I also knew that some of the light from our candles went not only out to the world but up into the night sky, through the atmosphere, single weak photons passing into infinite distances, fading from electromagnetic energy to spirit, sending to the Lord the prayers and hopes of a small group of followers of Christ on a small planet, that there might be healing of survivors and rebirth for the fractured church that had caused their suffering.

Father Tom stood at the top of the stairs with his hands raised, silver hair bright with the light of candles, against the dark sky. This holy and courageous priest, who had helped make the healing mass and our group possible, raised his hands and blessed us. When he did, we were enveloped by blissful silence.

Father Tom completed the evening by saying, "We wish all of you the gift of peace, the gift of healing."

Monsignor John Philbin, our beloved former pastor, who had predicted that the Holy Spirit would come with a sword to purify his church, a man who had been ordained a priest more than half a century ago, said that it was the most powerful liturgy he had ever attended.

CHAPTER 6

LIKE the MAN
in TIANANMEN SQUARE

— I —

AS VOICE OF THE FAITHFUL GREW rapidly, I became even more convinced that the perceptions of church leaders, and the public, about our intentions would depend to a large extent on how the media portrayed us. We had finally welcomed journalists to our meetings and we made it a point to keep those with interest in us well informed of our actions.

Indeed, an important, in-depth piece was published on page one of the *Boston Globe* on May 1, written by Michael Paulson, the newspaper's distinguished religion reporter. The article began:

In the basement of a parish school at Saint John the Evangelist Church, a quiet revolution is brewing.

A group that started three months ago as a listening session for parishioners upset about clergy sexual abuse has grown explosively in the past few weeks, drawing about 4,200 supporters from 36 states and 19 countries.

Each Monday night, hundreds of people are packing the Wellesley Hills church, so many that they can no longer fit into the school basement, so many that the group, called Voice of the Faithful, is starting to meet several nights a week and is considering finding a new home.

I was quoted in the article as saying, "If I had a dream of what this would look like three years from now, our enrollment would be half of the Catholics in the world, every parish would have a chapter, and every diocese, every nation, and the world would, too, and that our organization would be a counterbalance to the power of the hierarchy—it would have a permanent role, a bit like Congress." I continued, "My nightmare scenario is that the church successfully papers over the clergy sexual abuse problem and leaves intact an abusive power structure. . . . That's why we're moving so fast, why we're meeting three times a week now. Because we know we have to seize the moment."

A crucial point was made in the article by Steve Pope of Boston College, who was scheduled to speak at our next Voice meeting. He said, "There have always been people on the activist agenda who have wanted to change the church, either on the left or on the right, and who haven't had much impact. But this crisis has moved the broad middle of the church, people who have been pretty content and have been complacent. There are a lot of mainstream, middle-of-the road Catholics who are feeling called to be active in the church in a new way, and that's one of the significant elements of this crisis." Steve added: "I love the Catholic Church, but our fatal flaw has been the passivity of the laity."

This article, which so accurately described our movement, led to further press interest and triggered both increased attendance at our meetings and a dramatic surge in registrants on our Web site. And then one night Paul Baier arrived at a meeting with thrilling news. He'd checked our Web site hits and found something remarkable: Someone had accessed our site from— of all places—the Vatican.

They knew who we were.

— I I —

At our next meeting, held on a balmy Monday evening, the church basement was packed prior to our scheduled starting time of 7:30—so packed that scores of people were sent over to the parish hall, where we ran a parallel meeting. Throughout the night the other speakers and I shuttled back and forth so we could address both groups.

Mary Scanlon was chairing the meeting and she offered newcomers what I thought was a particularly apt description of our group. "When we learned that children had been mistreated, our hearts were broken," she said. "We had to come together to share our sorrow, our anger, and our shame. This violence happened to our children, in *our* church. What can we do to heal *our* children and our church?"

Mary then introduced Phil Saviano. Phil thought he had been invited to our meeting to simply sit in and listen, but when he arrived he learned that we hoped he would address the group. When Phil rose to speak, there was an easygoing charm about him, a straightforward manner suggesting that we would be hearing the uncensored truth.

Phil told us his story. He grew up in a small, rural town called East Douglas in Worcester County, Massachusetts. When he was eleven years old a new priest arrived in town, a charismatic man named Father David Holley. Father Holley was in his mid-thirties, a large man, six feet, two inches tall. He was outgoing and possessed an easy manner around children and always seemed to have a joke or card trick to amuse them. One day, Father Holley showed some card tricks to Phil and several of his friends using a deck of cards with sexually explicit pictures. After showing the card tricks—they were gathered just inside the front entrance to the church—Phil said Father Holley exposed himself to the boys. Soon thereafter, said Phil, Father Holley would take him to different parts of the church and require him to perform oral sex. While Phil did this in one part of the church, parishioners prayed in another.

Phil would think about trying to get out of it but he saw no possible way. He could not go to his parents—he knew that if he did that he would be blamed for it, not the priest. He felt trapped and defenseless.

And then one day, eighteen months after he had arrived, Father Holley was gone, without explanation. Phil Saviano was thrilled. He felt relieved, liberated. He was not consciously aware of how hurt he was for many years. In high school he was lonely and depressed. He made a feeble attempt at suicide, which left him alive yet scarred from a razor blade. But college at the University of Massachusetts at Amherst helped improve his life greatly.

Years passed. On December 17, 1991, when Phil was forty-one years old, he was looking over the newspaper ads in preparation for Christmas shopping. He saw a story about two young men who had been abused by a priest in New Mexico. The priest was Father David Holley.

Phil gasped. He felt as though he had been struck by lightning. Working through a legendary reporter at the *Globe*, Stephen Kurkjian, Phil got in touch with the abuse victims in

New Mexico. One of the victims had been molested when he was only eight years old! The two men there had gone to the New Mexico hierarchy to report the abuse but they had been turned away—and now they had filed a lawsuit. Phil discovered that Father Holley had been convicted of rape and sentenced to 275 years in prison—the longest sentence ever given to a Catholic priest in America.

Phil went public with his story in the belief that it could help others. In an effort to get the facts out he filed suit against the Worcester diocese. He was pressured to sign a secrecy agreement—one so restrictive it would have prevented Phil from speaking to his family and friends about the matter. He refused to sign. "I knew that bottling this all up would be emotionally harmful to me," he said. He also felt that if he signed the confidentiality agreement he would be "part of the conspiracy of silence."

In the course of his research, Phil learned that Father Holley had been discovered by his superiors in several assignments; that he had been sent off to treatment centers and then put right back into parishes where he continued to have access to children. Parishes where he was sent were never warned of his predatory past. Phil learned that six bishops in four states "knew he was a child molester" and continued to permit him to work.

Phil eventually won out. He was not required to sign a confidentiality agreement, and he received, from the Roman Catholic Archdiocese of Worcester, a settlement totaling

$12,500. He told us that he had been involved with the issue of priest sexual abuse for ten years and yet this was the very first time any Catholic organization had invited him to speak.

"It's a great honor for me and I want to thank you, but I can't help but wonder why it took so long." The entire crowd was riveted. Then everyone burst into applause and stood cheering him, a thunderous ovation. It was an emotional moment for Phil, vindication for which he had hoped for many years, and he fought back tears. He felt an outpouring of respect for what he had done, for his courage and determination—for the fact that he had survived and fought on.

—∿—

Steve Pope of Boston College followed Phil's presentation, which was not an easy thing to do. However, he immediately captured our attention when he began with a quote from Pope John Paul II in a document published in 1999 entitled *Ecclesia in America,* which stated: "The renewal of the Church in America will not be possible without the active presence of the laity. Therefore, they are largely responsible for the future of the Church."

We were eager to hear such affirmation. Steve, a distinguished theologian, said that Vatican II clearly embraced the notion of meaningful lay involvement in church affairs. Indeed, Vatican Council II was at the heart of our movement. Convened by Pope John XXIII in Rome from the fall of 1962 until December 1965, it was the largest such gathering in church history.

The council resulted in a number of reforms—the most noted being the shift from the mandatory Latin Mass to celebrating the liturgy in one's native language. The council produced various documents, including *The Dogmatic Constitution on the Church* (*Lumen Gentium*), which defined certain rights and responsibilities of lay people. Vatican II resulted, as well, in a philosophical split between conservatives, who considered the reforms too far reaching, and liberals, who believe that the church has not adequately instituted the reforms that were proposed.

Vatican II, Steve said, advanced the idea that the church, as the Body of Christ, includes *all* the people and not just the hierarchy. He quoted church writings explicitly stating that the members of the laity are obliged to offer their opinion on matters that concern the good of the church. While the hierarchy plays a special role in teaching and governing within the church, he said it is not an exclusive role. He said that working with the hierarchy was desirable but that we need not accept every judgment from the hierarchy. He quoted Dorothy Day as saying that with the church "one must live in a state of permanent dissatisfaction."

— I I I —

For Voice, a major event was on the horizon—our meeting with Bishop Edyvean. A week or so beforehand, I prepared some notes on the goals for our meeting. I wanted to convey to him that our mission, reached through consensus, was to provide a prayerful Voice, attentive to the Spirit, through which the Faithful can actively participate in the guidance and governance of the Church. Above all I wanted to convey to him that we wanted to help; that our purpose was to work cooperatively with other groups and with the hierarchy to resolve the problems plaguing the Roman Catholic Archdiocese of Boston and the universal church.

Strategically, I thought we were in a strong position going into the meeting. We had been growing rapidly and receiving widespread press coverage—virtually all of it favorable. We were emerging in the press as an important new voice of the Catholic laity. Unlike other Catholic groups, we had never taken a position on controversial issues such as married priests, women's ordination, and birth control. In retrospect, it seemed a great bit of good fortune that we had not voted in favor of the Cardinal's resignation. Had we done so, it is unlikely that Bishop Edyvean would have agreed to meet with us.

During a steering committee discussion a couple of weeks prior to the meeting, we talked about who should represent our group. It was quickly agreed that Mary Scanlon and I—as vice president and president—would attend. But we weren't sure who the third member of our delegation should be. Both Steve Krueger and Jim Post were strong possibilities. Jim was a business school professor and lawyer, an articulate, worldly man who worked well with people. Steve was a devout Catholic whose passion and sincerity were obvious. In front of the steering committee, both Jim and Steve gave a brief example of the types of things they would be inclined to say at the meeting with Bishop Edyvean. It was clear that while Jim's tone was polite, his message was firm. Steve's tone was more collegial, his message more conciliatory. He said he did not want to go into the meeting leading with his anger.

"Steve, the difference between you and me is that I'm angrier than you are," Jim cheerfully acknowledged.

Steve also had the advantage of having been active in diocesan affairs for many years so he knew Bishop Edyvean and other leaders at the chancery. In fact, Steve had spoken with the Cardinal during a meeting of the Archdiocesan Pastoral Council several weeks earlier. During a break in the meeting, Steve had approached Cardinal Law and asked whether he would be willing to meet with representatives from Voice of the Faithful. Law had said he couldn't do that. He said that Voice people had picketed his residence and the group had called for his resignation. Steve replied that some individual members of Voice may have joined picketers outside the chancery, but they had not done it as a sanctioned act on behalf of Voice as a group. And he told the Cardinal that we had not, in fact, formally called for his resignation.

"Really?" said the Cardinal, clearly interested in what Steve was saying. He told Steve he would speak with Bishop Edyvean about the matter and the Cardinal did so, which helped to facilitate our meeting. Steve was chosen as the third member of our delegation.

As the day of the meeting approached, our anticipation grew. We saw this as a wonderful opportunity to begin a dialogue with the hierarchy. Yet we knew this would not be a quick or easy marriage. There had been unsettling signs all along concerning the Boston hierarchy's relationship with the laity, and recently there had even been some disturbing developments. Just a couple of weeks earlier, on behalf of the Cardinal, Bishop Edyvean had written a letter to all the parishes ordering priests to suppress the formation of an association of Parish Pastoral Councils. Parish councils generally include the most active and devoted members of each parish. David W. Zizik, a lawyer who had once made a pilgrimage to Rome with the Cardinal, had sought to knit together an association of such councils from throughout the archdiocese as a way for lay people to communicate more effectively with the hierarchy. David had sent an e-mail to a variety of Catholic activists enunciating his rationale for the association.

"The absence of meaningful relationships between laity and hierarchy within our Church," he wrote, "and the presence of what appears to be a culture of insularity and secrecy within the hierarchy, are matters that lay faithful should and must be concerned with, because they have contributed directly to the creation of the child abuse problem within our Church and, unless remedied, will continue to cause damage to the Church in the future."

But the Cardinal directed Bishop Edyvean to suppress Zizik's efforts. Bishop Edyvean wrote that the Cardinal "does not endorse or recognize the proposed association. As pastor or parochial vicar, you are not to join, foster, or promote this endeavor among your parish pastoral council members or the community of the faithful at large."

The bishop wrote that there were four "canonically recognized bodies within the Archdiocese which aid the Archbishop in his role of governance. These are the Presbyteral Council (a council of priests), the College of Consultors, the Archdiocesan Finance Council, and the Archdiocesan Pastoral Council. The latter represents the People of God of the Archdiocese (c. 512) and renders the proposed Association superfluous and potentially divisive. Discussions have begun and will be extended on the topic of how to make the canonically recognized groups more effective in the Archdiocese."

The difficulty here, of course, was that these groups were formed and controlled by the Cardinal. They possessed no independence. The nature of all these groups was subservience, and we were past that. The sexual abuse crisis and the cover-up by the hierarchy *demanded* that we get past that. Subservience had helped create the environment in which the crisis could occur.

Zizik told reporters, "It's astounding to me that this church seems to be so afraid of dialogue with its own members, people who love it and who would give almost anything to see the church get back on track. This is a church that's supposed to invite the disenfranchised in—Jesus invited prostitutes and tax cheats—so it's almost bizarre to see the response of our church leadership. There is a pathology in our church that needs to be rooted out, and people are going to begin to vote with their feet if we don't do something about it."

At the time of the attack on Zizik's proposed association, Voice was not yet under assault, probably because we had arisen from the people publicly. In contrast, the parish councils were established by the hierarchy and hence a more likely target for control at the slightest hint of insubordination.

Another discouraging sign came a few days before our meeting with Bishop Edyvean when one of our leaders received an e-mail from a priest friend. It read in part:

> I wanted to alert you and the group that priests who are trying to start a VOTF or similar groups on the parish level are receiving phone calls from Edyvean, at the request of the Cardinal, telling them to cease and desist immediately. . . .
>
> According to Canon Law, if a Bishop informs you not to engage in what he believes to be subversive activity, like dialoguing with your people, he must put it in writing. I have heard that they will

not resort to that method, since they are afraid the press will get a copy. So instead we get these secret late-night phone calls. . . . What a nightmare!

At the next meeting of a group called the Boston Priests Forum, I am going to raise the question as to why we as a priest group are remaining so silent. If one or two speak out, they are immediately confronted by Edyvean. However, if 200 priests can draft a petition, respectfully requesting the resignation of the Cardinal, what are they going to do? . . .

I put you on alert because my feeling is that the Hierarchy is trying their best to squelch the VOTF, and they are beginning this process with intimidation tactics first aimed at the clergy.

The day before the meeting with Bishop Edyvean I asked members of our steering committee to think of us the following afternoon at 3:30, and to say a prayer that we would have success. Going into the meeting, I thought the most desirable outcome would be that the bishop agree to support our organization. Short of that, success would be his acceptance of our help working with survivors or helping to raise money. At the very least, success would be his willingness to continue to talk with us.

It felt good to be going in with Steve Krueger and Mary Scanlon. Steve has a wonderful working knowledge of the local hierarchy, and Mary has a remarkable sense of compassion and caring, particularly for survivors.

Steve Krueger, a man in his early fifties, has an MBA and provided investment banking services for start-ups and financially distressed companies for many years but never felt defined by his work. He was searching for a more meaningful spiritual life. In 1991, while working on a turnaround in Minneapolis/St. Paul, Steve experienced what he describes as a spiritual awakening. It was a turning point in his life, and one that led him to a point where he began to see his life as a spiritual journey that had to be embraced. His reading list, and the focus of his life, shifted from management and finance to spiritual growth and the life of the church. Moving back to the Boston area where he grew up, he became active in a variety of activities within his parish. Soon, he was appointed to the Archdiocesan Pastoral Council, where he met with Cardinal Law numerous times over the four years leading up to Law's resignation.

Although his own parish experience was fulfilling, he felt the church was not providing the kind of nurturing people needed.

In 1997 Steve read the documents of Vatican II and found his life changing again. He vividly remembers reading of his baptismal rights and responsibilities, how we are all—by virtue of our baptism—a priestly people. He remembers thinking, "If I am not part of the solution to the problems of the Church, then I am part of the problem." He saw that it was the rightful place of lay persons to involve themselves in the life of the Church. "If the Church is not going to make opportunities for us to use our gifts in the life of the Church, then we will have to make those opportunities for ourselves." When the clergy sexual abuse crisis broke, Steve knew that the laity *had to do something.*

I had known Mary for many years and I always had a profound respect for her. She is a tall, robust woman with a great mane of thick wavy auburn hair, a woman who would never fail to be noticed in a crowd. She was fifty-six years old at the time with a ready smile and a warm, almost earth-mother aura. She is, in fact, the mother of five children as well as two grown stepchildren and the foster mother of a fifteen-year-old girl. Her penetrating gaze and breathy voice give her an air of intensity. Mary is the daughter of devout Catholic parents and she attended Catholic schools from the second grade through college. Soon after college she married and subsequently had five children. Her faith remained central to her life as she was raising her children Catholic. When she and her husband divorced, Mary went through the process of having the marriage annulled so that she would be conforming to Catholic rules.

Mary integrated her profession as a nurse-practitioner with her strong beliefs that she was called to help those who suffered. She had worked in a hospice setting where she felt immensely rewarded aiding families gathered to support their loved ones in the final hours of this life. Ever since the scandal broke she had thought often about the victims of abuse and how they had suffered. Her concern from the start was reaching out to survivors to let them know they are not alone and that there are people within the church who object to the treatment they had received.

"My primary feeling was as a mother thinking of a child being wronged and the child not having a place to go or someone to turn to. I wanted to say, 'This is wrong and we won't tolerate it.' I wanted to say to them, 'You were wronged but you are loved.'"

— I V —

The headquarters for the Archdiocese of Boston is set on a rolling campus in the Brighton neighborhood of Boston. The campus includes a half-dozen or so buildings, including a residence for Cardinal Law. The stone building, constructed early in the twentieth century, has the feeling of an Italian palazzo, with large rooms, high ceilings, and a sense of grandness. Critics of the Cardinal suggested that he should sell his opulent residence and give the money to survivors. We met in another chancery building, a fifties-era rectangular structure that was in no way grand.

As I described earlier, our meeting quickly became tense as we were accused of undermining the Cardinal. This led to the exchange in which we were able to confirm that Bishop Edyvean was indeed trying to block our efforts as we had been warned. After that, young Father O'Connell weighed in again, his tone hostile, accusing us of having called for the Cardinal's resignation. I said we had not done so; that although many of our members felt the Cardinal should resign, we as an organization had not endorsed the idea. I told him that on the night of the vote about the Cardinal I had led one of the most difficult meetings of my life; that I had insisted upon a rule that thwarted the will of 90 percent of our membership.

"You had no business even *considering* the question," Bishop Edyvean interrupted.

"Our members *wanted* to consider the question," I said, adding that we had every right to do so.

Mary Scanlon was surprised by the tone and direction of the meeting. She had come expecting Bishop Edyvean to be penitent. She thought he would admit the church had a problem. She thought we would go in with a good faith offer of assistance and the bishop would welcome our help. Mary listened in amazement as the bishop and young priest spoke, "giving the impression that they knew everything and we knew nothing."

Mary then spoke up. She wanted to convey to Bishop Edyvean how important the church was to her personally. She told of having gone through the shattering experience of divorce and then following through with the process of getting her marriage annulled. She said that it had been helpful to submit to the rules of the church. "It was a very healing process," she said. "It helped me move on."

She said that Voice had many members who were on parish council, served as lectors, sang in the choir, or taught religious education classes. They were deeply committed to the church, she assured the bishop, but wanted to deal with the scandal head-on. One way to do that, Steve interjected, was for us to help financially. Steve explained that we had established what we called a Voice of Compassion Fund to raise money from the many people who were unwilling to donate directly to the archdiocese. Steve explained that we wanted to donate the money we were raising to the archdiocese with the stipulation that it go to charitable rather than administrative costs.

This set Father O'Connell off yet again. He said we had no authority to raise money and we should not do it. We were amazed by this because we were well aware that donations to the archdiocese were down sharply as a result of the scandal. We were collecting money that people were not willing to give to the Cardinal's appeal.

I asked Father O'Connell why we shouldn't raise money intended for the poor. He said that the importance of the right relationship between the archbishop and his church takes primacy over funding the programs and ministries of the archdiocese. To emphasize the point, he said, "Principle is up here"—and he reached up with his left hand and held it above his head—"And money is down here"—and he reached down with his right hand, holding it way below the level of the table.

We were speechless. The notion that funds to care for the needy were subservient to an expansive definition of the Cardinal's power was insane; it was preposterous. We sat in silence, dumbfounded.

Mary said: "The dismal failure of the Cardinal's Appeal will mean that funds for the poor and needy in the archdiocese will be greatly reduced." Though Steve and I did not hear it, Mary says O'Connell's reply was clear: "Then they will have to go without." It was the most revealing moment of the meeting. For it was an admission that power was what truly mattered; the Cardinal must have the power to raise money and he would share that power with no one, even if the consequence was that the poor would suffer.

It was a scandalous statement, and Bishop Edyvean surely knew it. He added nuances and tried to soften what this arrogant young priest had said.

We returned to less controversial issues and sought to bring the meeting to a close. I suggested that we hold another meeting to see if we could find some common ground. Bishop Edyvean agreed. I raised the question of the media—there was a great deal of press interest in the fact that this meeting was being held. This led to our agreement that we would tell the press that we had a productive session and would soon meet again. Again, the bishop agreed.

We left the chancery at about 5:40 in the evening. A few minutes later, Mary was driving in her car when she received a call on her cell phone from a reporter seeking a comment on the meeting. He quoted the statement that had been issued by the archdiocese stating that the Cardinal's representative had reminded Voice that it was to operate only under the Cardinal's direction. Given our agreement to issue a joint statement, Mary was shocked to learn that this statement had already been issued by the archdiocese around 5:20 P.M.—while we were still in the meeting!

Mary felt we'd been *had*—completely blindsided. It was as though this were some sort of political campaign and the hierarchy was interested not in an honest dialogue about the crisis but in scoring points against us in the newspapers.

"It was my first personal experience of having been betrayed by the church," Mary said. "I was stunned."

— V —

The meeting with Bishop Edyvean left many of our members mightily discouraged. We learned, clearly, that we were not being embraced.

The next morning, the *Boston Herald* headline read: "BISHOP EXERTS CONTROL OVER NEW LAY GROUP." The article said, "Cardinal Bernard Law's top lieutenant yesterday asserted the right of the church hierarchy to oversee a powerful new organization of lay Roman Catholics."

While we were dismayed with this sort of positioning, there were positive aspects to the coverage as well. The lead paragraph characterized us as "a powerful new organization of lay Roman Catholics," which indicated that we had gained a certain stature with the press. The article also stated that our members "span a broad ideological spectrum." The story said that Voice was considered "a growing force in the U.S. church as lay Catholics seek more say given the failures in oversight of priests." And it announced our July convention.

The day after the meeting, once we had had a chance to absorb the press coverage and think it through, there was a flurry of reaction from within our group, mostly via e-mail. Peggie Thorp wrote:

> It strikes me as preposterous that any diocesan official should presume to preach on the mission of the Church when it is they who have assaulted that mission so brutally. On the plus side, we got a plug for the convention, a tag for our moderation, and a tone of balance and calm in our quoted statements. . . . The headline . . . lacks accuracy. This crisis remains about one thing to the diocese and, no doubt, the rest of the hierarchy—protect

the church at all/any cost. . . . In toto, we look good here and the diocese does not.

Terry McKiernan had the last word on the matter—at least for that day. Terry is bright and articulate and he had for some time been arguing that we were too passive; that we should take to the streets and join the protests of survivors. Terry wrote, "The chancery went into the meeting with a plan for spinning the meeting afterward. We just went to talk." Terry further wrote:

They didn't care what was said at the meeting. They planned to use the meeting to assert (or was it exert?) control over our movement, and [the hierarchy's] remarks were obviously prepared beforehand with this point in mind. . . .

We shouldn't be begging for meetings in which we have much to lose and they have lots to gain. And if we do meet . . . we need to remember that these are not nice people.

Edyvean is an old Vatican hand, and we have plenty of evidence that he intends to co-opt and crush the Voice. . . . Law and his administration have . . . put thousands of children at risk, intimidated victims, made pay-offs to buy silence, obstructed justice, and as of Pentecost Sunday, lied before God Himself. As a priest friend of ours has told us in plain English, when we deal with these people, we have to watch our backs.

Please, let's rethink this strategy.

While I shared the frustration of my friends, I also recognized that some positive things had come out of the meeting. I thought we had accomplished something important—that the mere fact of our meeting with the bishop helped to legitimize our organization, helped keep us very much in the public eye, and further showed that the hierarchy was being inflexible and insufficiently responsive to a mainstream lay organization. In addition, we could tell our members—and this would be particularly comforting to our more conservative members—that we were engaged in a dialogue with the hierarchy. There were Catholics who had drawn strength from the very fact of our meeting with Bishop Edyvean. Late that night I received an e-mail from a woman in another parish. She said that the priest there had received instructions from Edyvean to prevent the formation of a Voice of the Faithful chapter there. "Your inspired action has helped relieve their frustration and confusion. So, again, thank you for meeting with the Bishop and not cowering, and for all the rest of your tireless and devoted efforts."

There were other Catholics out there who noticed what we were doing and who believed in our mission. One was Terry Meehan, a New Yorker who cared deeply about his church and who wanted to help Voice. I had never met Terry, but he sent me an e-mail after reading about us in the press. Terry wrote his admiration of what we trying to do to help the church, and asked if he could be of assistance. I called him and we talked about Voice. I said our greatest need at the moment was for money to start an office. He said his family wanted to help and that he would send money. We soon received a check from Terry for $100,000. The Spirit—with help from the Meehans—was moving us forward.

Yet, it was becoming clearer with each passing day that our vision to create a lay organization that would work hand in hand with the hierarchy to get the church to a better place was not even slightly shared by some church leaders. Their desire was to continue the autocracy; to make all the decisions and to exclude us from any meaningful role. It meant we would have to get stronger, gain more independent power, and force them to pay attention to us. They did not want to hear our anger over the scandal and cover-up. They did not want to engage in a dialogue with us about the scandal or any other issue, for that matter. They did not want to hear our ideas for how to deal with survivors or how to raise money for the needy. And they *certainly* didn't want to hear our thoughts on restructuring the church to enable a greater voice and power for laity. So we would need to get stronger.

Our efforts in that direction were greatly helped on the last day of May, when our movement was described in a front-page article in the *New York Times* headlined "ANGRY AT SCANDAL, LAY GROUP SEEKS QUIET UPRISING IN PEWS." It described one of our meetings: "The room was charged with the nervous electricity of people plotting a revolution, in this case one that would change the very structure of the Roman Catholic Church so that lay people would have a voice in major decisions."

The article quoted R. Scott Appleby, a theologian at Notre Dame, who said, "This is one of the best possibilities for genuine reform in the church, precisely because this movement up to this point has not fallen into one of the categories that could allow it to be marginalized by the archdiocese." He continued, "Voice of the Faithful is very shrewd to be calling for reform based on principles in place already. They are Erasmus, not Luther. Erasmus said, 'I remain Catholic because I believe the basic theology of the church but I think there's widespread need for invigorating those institutions.'"

The piece ended with this:

> Sister Jon Julie Sullivan, a nun from Cambridge who attended a recent meeting, was impressed by the group's efforts to be "collaborative" with the archdiocese.
>
> "Of course the hierarchy is noticing," she said. "It's like the man in Tiananmen Square in front of the tank. It's a very strong image."

CHAPTER 7

RESISTANCE FROM BISHOPS, SUPPORT FROM THEOLOGIANS AND CLERGY

— I —

WHILE WE WERE MAKING little progress with the local hierarchy in Boston, the world's largest group of Catholic theologians issued a statement supporting the foundation of our activities. The group, the Catholic Theological Society of America, which includes as members many lay men and women and priests and nuns who work as teachers and professors, called for "thoroughgoing church reform" in light of the sexual abuse scandal and cover-up. They told reporters that "public outrage has been directed not just toward the instances of clerical sexual abuse themselves, but toward church leadership's systemic failure to maintain, even minimally, the kind of open communication, consultation and participative decision-making that ought to characterize the church."

One of the theologians stated emphatically: "We are clearly in a crisis that requires the laity to demand accountability from the bishops." It was a striking statement that went to the heart of our aspirations.

The second week of June 2002 offered Voice an opportunity to seek accountability from more than three hundred bishops from throughout the United States as they gathered in Dallas to discuss the sexual abuse crisis. We decided to send a three-person delegation to the meeting, composed of Paul Baier, Tanya Chermak, and Mike Emerton, who was now managing our press relations.

Terry McKiernan, an early participant in Voice, conducted a detailed study of the draft resolutions the bishops would debate. Terry is a brilliant man who had been taught by Franciscan nuns in grammar school and Jesuits in high school (Fordham Prep in the Bronx). He was a classicist who specialized in Homer and Greek lyric poetry. Terry's analytical mind was wonderfully suited to pore through the minutiae of the bishops' charter.

Under the terms of the draft, Terry determined, the bishops were, in effect, granting themselves amnesty. They were not admitting any wrongdoing, and even those who had knowingly transferred pedophiles could continue to enjoy a privileged life and secure retirement. All of this while the survivors suffered.

Terry observed that in 1985 and again in 1992 the bishops addressed the sexual abuse issue, yet very little had changed. In fact, on the eve of the current conference the *Dallas Morning News* reported that *two-thirds* of American bishops had transferred a known abuser! It was Terry's view, supported by many others at Voice, that there should be not only lay involvement in implementation of plans to deal with the sexual abuse issue, but the involvement of survivors as well. And both survivors and other lay people should be selected by means independent of the hierarchy.

Paul Baier was incensed that the draft of the Dallas Charter did not assign any responsibility to the bishops. "Are pew Catholics to understand that bishops had *no* culpability for this scandal?" he asked.

Our delegation was well prepared to describe Voice of the Faithful as well as to advance the issue of accountability of bishops. Our team arrived in Dallas on Thursday, June 13, checking into the Bradford Suites Hotel for $85 per night (in contrast to Cardinal Law, who arrived in Dallas by private jet and was escorted by a phalanx of security to his hotel).

The bishops' meeting was private—no press allowed—but they did plan an elaborate press conference for Friday, June 14.

Mike Emerton suggested that Voice hold a press conference two hours *before* the bishops. With such timing our message would be heard first and we could raise the important questions that we felt the bishops should address. We even managed to secure a function room in the same hotel, right down the hall from where the bishops' press conference would be held. Working feverishly to assemble press kits, Mike, Paul, and Tanya—with the help of Tanya's eleven-year-old son Alex—wrote on Mike's laptop and then printed out our documents in the business center of the hotel. As the reporters showed up for our event, Alex checked them in at the door and handed them a press kit.

Paul, Mike, and Tanya stood up at the podium and looked out at two dozen or more reporters and eight to ten television cameras. There were reporters from the *Boston Globe* and the *Boston Herald, USA Today*, the *Dallas Morning News*, the *Tampa Tribune*, the *Washington Post*, the *Miami Herald*, the San Jose *Mercury News*, and more. Mike and then Paul spoke as the video cams whirred and the still cameras flashed. They explained that the 1985 Vatican report had already identified the sex abuse problem and that the report had been sent to all the bishops. (Ironically, one of the authors of the report—Father Tom Doyle— would be the keynote speaker at our upcoming convention.) The existence of the Doyle-Mouton report, which detailed the sexual abuse in the church and predicted dire financial consequences unless the church moved to solve the problem, was unknown to most reporters. The news of it clearly captured their attention.

Paul and Mike noted that a decade earlier, at the U.S. Bishops conference, the bishops discussed the sexual abuse issue and stated that the problem was fixed. Yet in the next ten years, child molesters like Shanley and others were transferred, given access to children, and supplied with glowing letters of recommendation. The message was clear: The bishops had known since 1985, with reinforcement in 1992, that sexual abuse was a major problem within the Catholic Church and yet it had not been adequately addressed.

Paul Baier said the history of neglect by some bishops must now end. "We don't want another ten years to go by without anything done," he said.

"We've lost our moral and spiritual leadership," Tanya told the reporters. "We've had a disconnect with the behavior of our hierarchy. This movement is about lay people not sitting back and being treated like children anymore. It's time to make our voices heard in a meaningful way."

Mike, Paul, and Tanya said that they hoped our group's message would be conveyed to the bishops through the media. One reporter clearly was puzzled by this. "Are you telling me that you have no communications with the bishops? Don't they already know your concerns?" He was amazed that we were not in regular contact with the bishops.

Mike was careful to differentiate our group from other Catholic lay organizations. He explained that we were focused on gaining greater lay involvement in the church and that we deliberately did not take positions on controversial issues such as women's ordination, divorce, birth control, and celibacy. He also noted that as an organization we did not participate in demonstrations.

"We are committed to working within the system," Mike told the reporters. "This is what makes us different from many of the other organizations."

Paul and Mike talked about possibly using the power of the checkbook as a "lever of last resort" to compel the hierarchy to listen to us. Paul noted that there had been a drop in donations in the Archdiocese of Boston—a decline that threatened to harm countless needy people who relied upon Catholic charitable services. He then explained that we had launched our own fund-raising initiative as a way to compensate for some of that shortfall.

Mike said it was important that lay people participate in critical areas of church governance such as personnel, finance, and administration. "All we are asked to do now is pray, pay, and obey," Mike said. "A leveling of the power is absolutely necessary."

Tanya said she had come to Dallas to voice her objection to the "abuse of power" by church leaders. She said she thought that the sex abuse scandal and cover-up were so egregious that there was a risk of losing "a whole generation of Catholics" and in the process jeopardizing "the future of the church that we love." As a Catholic mother of two boys—eleven and fourteen—she thought it was imperative that she demonstrate Voice's commitment to survivors.

On the day after our press conference, all three members of our delegation were quoted extensively throughout the country. The favorable coverage increased interest and membership in Voice of the Faithful. Even in stories in which we weren't quoted directly, it was clear that our team had had an impact on the direction of the coverage. *USA Today* quoted the leader of the bishops' organization but also noted in the article that "missing from his comments, however, was any mention of repercussions for bishops who have ignored or covered up abuse or do so in the future. That's a priority of victims and lay groups, including the Survivors Network of those Abused by Priests (SNAP), the 25,000-member laity group Call To Action, and another reform group, Voice of the Faithful, based in Boston."

— I I —

On June 20, just five days after our delegation returned from Dallas, we had a private meeting with four leaders of the Boston Priest's Forum, a group of more than one hundred parish priests that had formed the year before the news of the abuse scandal broke. The purpose of the forum, several of the priests had stated publicly, was to create "a place for us to do theological and moral reflection in an open and dynamic environment of our peers."

They said in a public statement defining their group that "the current crisis and the way it has been handled are symptoms of a deeper crisis facing the church, a crisis that has triggered forces that have long been restive. The question now is how will these forces for change be met? Will it be with wisdom and authentic leadership or will the church cling to ways of operating that have proven fragile, unreliable, and outdated?"

A number of members of Voice were close to some of the Priest's Forum participants. After a series of conversations it was agreed that the leadership of the Priest's Forum would come to one of our steering committee meetings. We wanted the meeting to be confidential, for if word got back to the cardinal that four parish priests were meeting with us there would surely be anger and perhaps recriminations against them. This very notion was disturbing. The idea that priests and lay Catholics gathering together would be viewed with displeasure or suspicion by the hierarchy had medieval overtones. Steve Krueger thought of it as kind of "cloak and dagger—in the back room of a back room in a dark place in Budapest."

The meeting was held at St. Bernard's in Newton and included Fathers Robert Bullock, Walter Cuenin, Gerry Osterman, and Paul Kilroy. All were in their sixties, perhaps one or two approaching seventy; all were widely known to be men of honor and distinction.

Father Bob Bullock was the leader, tall and angular, craggy in a New England way with a long thin face and snow-white hair. Father Bullock seemed exceptionally fit for a man his age, perhaps due to his background as a runner who had completed the Boston Marathon. In contrast to Father Bullock, Father Walter Cuenin was a roundish man who had a perpetual smile on his face and a lightning wit. Father Gerry Osterman was tall and distinguished looking with a shock of white hair. Father Paul Kilroy had a wide-open face with a warm, welcoming expression. The evening was warm and all four were dressed casually in open-necked golf shirts. Fathers Kilroy and Cuenin wore Bermuda shorts and Cuenin had on deck shoes without socks. That they wore street clothes meant a lot to us. It suggested that they were joining us as colleagues, friends.

Our steering committee was excited about this meeting because for the first time we were in dialogue with a priests' group. We knew these priests to be among the finest in the archdiocese. That they were also among the activist movers and shakers in the archdiocese lent gravity to the meeting. It was enormously affirming that they would take the time to travel from their parishes to meet with us. It was yet another indication of our mounting influence.

We gathered in the basement of the church and sat in a circle, two dozen or more members of our steering committee and four priests trying to determine how best the groups could find common purpose. Father Bullock told us that the members of the Priest's Forum were very supportive of the work Voice was doing and urged us to keep pushing, to grow our numbers. "You need to know how much we need you," Father Bullock said. He urged us to "say what you have to say" and observed that we were in a position of freedom—we could say and do things that they could not.

Father Bullock and the others were quite candid in saying that they did not feel as though their voices were heard by the hierarchy either, that through the years they had felt a chill emanating from the chancery. There was not a great deal of effort by church leaders to be supportive of the priests out there in the vineyards. Rather, there had been an aloofness, a sense of arrogance and condescension.

One of the priests said that he believed the time had come to "explain our message of being together, of developing trust between laity, hierarchy, and clergy, and of taking risks without apology and without fear." There was a difference, he said, "between being respectful of hierarchy and being deferential."

Father Bullock—followed by his colleagues—expressed concern about our goal of supporting "priests of integrity." They were uncomfortable with that language. The issue for Father Bullock and the others was that the second goal seemed purely in the context of the first—in other words, the message seemed to be that priests of integrity were defined as those who did not engage in sexual abuse, period. But Father Bullock believed that the definition of integrity for a priest was far broader—that a priest of integrity was one who tells the truth, who does not put ambition ahead of truth, and who lives by the

Gospel. They suggested that we change our wording to support priests in their ministry, rather than priests of integrity. We said that we would discuss the possibility.

When it came time for the priests to leave, I walked them outside as the meeting continued inside. Out on the sidewalk, the issue of our planning to have a mass at our convention came up. Father Bullock said that no mass could be celebrated in the archdiocese without approval from the chancery. Father Bullock and the other priests cautioned us not to go ahead with a mass. They suggested that we might consider a para-liturgy—an event that would not be a sacrament but that would be something like a mass, only run by laity. Father Osterman warned that we should not do anything "outside the liturgical norms. That's something Cardinal Law sees red about." The priests urged our group to "make sure women didn't do anything that wasn't already allowed." Father Osterman said that if our goal was to be in communication with the powers-that-be in the archdiocese, then it was important "to be cautious on the liturgical thing or it will come back to bite you."

The priests pressed the idea of a prayer service, which would not require the permission of the cardinal and could include many lay men and women. I thought that solution made some sense but I also thought it was essential that Susan Troy, who was in charge of the worship services at the convention, participate in our discussion. I went back inside and asked her to come outside for a moment. When she joined us in the sweltering heat of the night, I told her that I, too, was concerned that we could face some conflict with the hierarchy if we pushed for a mass. But, to her credit, Susan was immovable. "We have to have a mass. You can't put four thousand Catholics together and not celebrate the Eucharist!" The Eucharist is at the center of our faith, she said. We must have a mass. Father Bullock was struck by the resolute position that Susan took along with Svea and others. "There was no question in their minds they going to have mass," Bullock said later.

Father Bullock said, "If she wants to do it, we have to support her."

"It turned out to be a coming-of-age moment," Susan Troy remembered later. "The Eucharist belongs to all of us. It's not one of the assets of the Roman Catholic Archdiocese of Boston."

— I I I —

Our second meeting with Bishop Edyvean occurred on June 26, a month after the first. Mary Scanlon and Steve Krueger and I were joined by another Voice member, Bill Cadigan, who contributed his executive skills as vice president of Voice. We were shown into the same imposing conference room in which we had met earlier. The bishop arrived in the room with Father O'Connell and another priest, whom he introduced as Father Oliver, another canon lawyer, who appeared to be in his forties.

This time, we started by expressing our concern. I told the bishop that their issuance of a press release at variance with our mutual agreement on what we would say about the previous meeting had caused great discord within our group. It reinforced the hand of those who said we could not trust the Boston hierarchy and wanted us to end our discussions.

The bishop immediately began backpedaling from the incident. He said he was not in charge of press releases and wasn't aware that that had happened.

We said that it could not happen again. If there was to be a statement issued to the press after the meeting, it had to be a joint effort. Otherwise it would be necessary for us to leave.

Bishop Edyvean agreed that we would prepare a joint statement. Father Oliver then lectured us on the relationship of the archbishop to the church and the sorts of associations the laity were permitted to form.

But we'd done our homework. We had researched and studied and, most important, consulted with canon lawyers and theologians and we knew that we were on solid ground in our effort to exist independently of the hierarchy. Our ability to do this was clearly enunciated within canon law and documents from Vatican II. I said we were an independent organization yet we wanted to work closely and in concert with the hierarchy. "We have come seeking the Cardinal's support. We would like the Cardinal to acknowledge us and to support our efforts to form affiliates in other parishes."

We said that we wanted more effective and democratic channels through which the laity could participate in the church. Bishop Edyvean replied that there were already established means for lay involvement in the life of the diocese—namely the archdiocesan finance and pastoral councils, and parish pastoral and finance councils. Steve Krueger, Mary, and Bill had all served on one or more of those panels, and we said that there were severe limitations to these bodies. We suggested that there should be a representative body of laity—*elected by laity.*

The bishop then sought to minimize our standing in the community by pointing out that while we had a grand total of 16,000 members, there were 2.3 million Catholics in the Archdiocese of Boston alone. I countered by saying we were a young organization and that we were growing rapidly. I also wondered what percent of those 2.3 million would side with the Cardinal.

As the meeting progressed, I noticed that Father O'Connell was as mute in this meeting as he had been voluble in the first. I wondered if Bishop Edyvean had counseled moderation after his comments in the first meeting. But whatever arrogance was missing from Father O'Connell was more than supplied by Father Oliver. He instructed us at some length about the imperative of our being subservient to the archbishop. He said he had five or six problems with Voice of the Faithful.

"That's fine," I said. "If you have these questions about us then please come to our convention and raise the questions and we'll discuss them. We want to do this right." I specifically said we would welcome the three of them to our convention as well as the Cardinal and anyone else from the chancery who might wish to join us. From where we sat at that moment, the Hynes Convention Center was only a fifteen-minute car ride, and they would be most welcome. But there was no indication from any of them that they would accept our invitation.

At one point, Father Oliver said that revelation is given to the hierarchy. Mary Scanlon objected. "I believe God reveals himself to all of us in different ways. God reveals himself in family experiences and work experiences and as laity we have special wisdom that comes from being a lay person."

Father Oliver said that wasn't the main source of the revelation. He said that God was revealed primarily through the hierarchy and the hierarchy was in a position to translate revelation to lay people.

I spoke about Vatican II and told them that we were faithful Catholics who wanted to help. Mary echoed what I was saying: "We're not a threat," she said. "We're here to help."

But once again their reaction indicated that they didn't want our help. They clearly wanted to have control over us and we just as clearly were not going to be controlled by them.

Mary made an impassioned plea on behalf of survivors. She had made it a point to reach out and meet with numerous survivors and she told the bishop that. She said she considered the survivors to be "the presence of Christ in the world today." She said that they "have a special understanding of Christ's suffering, death, and Resurrection because they were innocents who were betrayed, underwent the deadening of their spirits, and have made the journey back to life." She said that survivors had contacted Cardinal Law's office requesting meetings to discuss the possibilities for healing but were rebuffed.

Bishop Edyvean said that the Cardinal was willing to meet with victims and that there would be an increased effort to set up such meetings—except for those in litigation against the archdiocese. Mary said that we at Voice believed that it was the responsibility of the archdiocese to pay for counseling services for victims. She said that the archdiocese offered counseling but that it required victims to report abuse details that then become available to the archdiocesan lawyers and to church officials. The bishop said that there would be such independent counseling set up very soon.

We were pleased at that bit of progress, but then came a somewhat stunning moment. Bishop Edyvean looked at me and said: "You have an image problem," meaning Voice of the Faithful. It was breathtaking. Here was a man who was part of a hierarchy that had permitted priests to sexually abuse children and then covered it up—and he was claiming that *we* had an image problem!

"The hierarchy has the image problem, Bishop Edyvean," I said. "Not us."

But he insisted that among conservative Catholics we did have a problem because they perceived Voice as too liberal.

Steve Krueger was upset by the bishop's tone. The intent of the meeting, Steve thought, was to have a dialogue, but we were being lectured to. "You seem to think the problem you need to face is how you can regain the trust of the laity," Steve said. "But the real problem you face is how to trust the laity for the first time." Bishop Edyvean did not disagree. He said, "We may have to do both."

But perhaps the most surprising moment of the meeting occurred when I told Bishop Edyvean and Fathers Oliver and O'Connell about our plans to hold a mass at the end of our convention.

There was a silence in the room. Then Bishop Edyvean smiled and looked at Oliver and O'Connell and spoke a sentence in Latin. After he had done so, the three of them laughed.

I am fluent in Russian, but I hadn't taken Latin since the tenth grade and so I wasn't certain what he had said.

As we left, Mary whispered to us: "Did you catch what he said? '*Silentium assensum dat.*' Silence gives consent."

So while they'd been arrogant and condescending, they hadn't said no to our plans for a mass.

We left the meeting with mixed feelings. No, they had not embraced us or endorsed us. No, they would not promote the spread of Voice affiliates to other parishes. But the bishop had agreed to meet again, and he had said he would try and facilitate a meeting for us with the financial people at the chancery. That struck us as significant. We had no idea that the planned meeting with the archdiocesan financial people would not occur and that we would not meet again with Bishop Edyvean for many months.

In retrospect, I am struck by the sequence of events over that two-week-plus period. There was the triumph of Dallas, where our group was a powerful public voice on the policies being debated by the bishops. There was the uplifting meeting with the members of the Boston Priest's Forum. And now, just days later, there was this—back to business as usual.

Toward the end of the meeting we had discussed what to do about the press. Bishop Edyvean said that in the next day or so we should get in touch with the spokesperson for the archdiocese. We put together a proposed joint statement that included this sentiment: "It is hoped this dialogue will identify a range of acceptable solutions that would establish the trust for a collaborative and participatory structure of the church—envisioned by the Second Vatican Council—the implementation of which would permit the Church to move forward in a stronger and more capable position to fulfill its mission."

We pursued the archdiocesan press person for days afterward, but without success. The planned joint statement was never issued.

It was now crystal clear that the Boston hierarchy wanted us to go away.

CHAPTER 8

A MIRACULOUS
CONVENTION

— I —

OUR ORGANIZATION WAS GROWING rapidly, and so too were the expectations for our upcoming convention. When Paul Baier originally proposed the idea back in March 2002, we had been an organization of a few hundred people. Now, in June, as the convention approached, we had grown to a movement of nineteen thousand members in forty states and twenty-one countries. Our rapid growth was fueled by a desire on the part of thousands of Catholics to do *something* in response to the sex abuse scandal. And Voice of the Faithful was clearly positioned as a responsible, mainstream way to respond. Catholics joined Voice through a welcoming, synergistic combination of personal contacts, e-mail, publicity, and our Web site. Our weekly meetings were so moving that attendees usually returned and often brought new members with them. Participants then informed friends of the "happenings" via e-mail and phone and directed them to our Web site, where it was easy for them to join our e-mail list. We established a core group of volunteers to attempt to reply to the flood of contacts.

With our large list of supporters from all over the world, it was clear to me that we had much to gain from the convention—but we had much to lose as well. I had told a reporter from the *Los Angeles Times* that our intention was to "serve as a voice for mainstream Catholics and create a mechanism for democracy." The *Times* said of Voice that "[t]he test of their strength" would come with the convention.

Our ambitions were great. We wanted to fill the Hynes Convention Center on July 20 and show the world that in the wake of the sex abuse scandal, a group of Catholic lay people committed to acknowledging the truth and changing the church could come together with a strong, common voice. Several people pointed out that our meeting had the potential to be the largest gathering of self-organized lay Catholics to convene in the country in many years.

By the end of June dozens of media outlets registered to cover the event, including the *New York Times*, the *Washington*

Post, National Public Radio, the major television networks, and reporters from throughout the United States and Europe.

The event, which Paul Baier started by himself with his energy and commitment, had now become a massive, complex endeavor. Paul had anticipated the complexity and managed the process with great skill. He hired and worked closely with a professional event planner, Ann Schaeffer, who was Catholic and agreed to work for a modest amount of money. Paul and Ann, with the help of hundreds of volunteers, planned for countless logistical challenges.

We selected a very basic structure for the convention: There would be a plenary session in the morning with several speakers; breakout sessions on a variety of topics would follow lunch; then there would be an additional plenary session followed by mass.

Bill Fallon, who was in charge of the speakers, quickly lined up an impressive array of theologians and academics and, with the help of Mary Scanlon, he added a number of survivors to the list as well. Since the beginning of Voice, I had pushed hard to make sure we were an inclusive group. While most of our members were moderate-to-liberal Catholics, we also had a small but critical contingent of conservatives. To make sure that all points of view were presented, I wanted a number of conservatives as speakers at the convention.

"We sent out invitations to conservative Catholics like George Weigel," Bill Fallon recalled. Bill called Weigel's office and the phone "rang and rang and rang and rang and then finally there was a pick-up and a voice gruffly said, 'Weigel.' When I identified myself, he said, 'VOTF—I know all about *you*. I'm not available.'" We invited a number of other conservatives as well, but all turned us down.

Meanwhile, the timing of the convention was turning out to be perfect. As more and more Catholics saw our determined approach as a way to act in response to the scandal, the pace of ticket sales quickened. We also realized that just about everyone who bought a $20 ticket also made an additional donation to Voice. When Susan Troy needed $1,000 for hosts for communion, Paul Baier put out the word that he needed a $1,000 gift for hosts, and in response, received five such gifts. This sort of affirmation was enormously energizing to our group, for it was an unmistakable sign that we had struck a deep chord with many Catholics. In all, by the time the convention arrived, we had raised $80,000 from the sale of tickets and had received additional donations of $80,000—including Paul Baier's gift of $10,000.

—⁓—

Media coverage began several days before the convention. James Carroll, a former priest and distinguished author of both fiction and nonfiction, wrote a column in the *Globe* four days before the convention suggesting that "next Saturday may well mark the beginning of a new era in the Catholic Church." He wrote,

"Thousands of Catholic lay people will gather at the Hynes Convention Center in Boston to respond to the catastrophe caused by priests abusing children and by bishops protecting abusers instead of victims."

Carroll enunciated what would be an essential theme running throughout our convention. He said we would be "fulfilling the mandate laid out [for laity] at Vatican II; 'By reason of the knowledge, competence, or preeminence which they have,' the council fathers declared, 'the laity are empowered—indeed sometimes obliged—to manifest their opinion on those things which pertain to the good of the church.'"

As he so often does in his columns, Carroll got to the heart of the matter:

> Here is the irony: Vatican II did establish in principle the rights and responsibilities of the Catholic laity to exercise power in the church, and now, against the prevailing opinion of the present hierarchy, the laity must claim that power and thereby rescue what was begun a generation ago. The very definition of the church is at stake. Does the church consist of the pope, bishops, and priests, with lay people as a kind of auxiliary underclass? Or is the church, in Vatican II's term, "the people of God"? Just by convening on its own authority, the Voice of the Faithful community will answer that question.

The next morning—three days prior to the convention—Michael Paulson of the *Globe* weighed in with an article headlined "NEW CATHOLIC REFORM GROUPS AT A CROSSROADS." The article raised the prospect that the Cardinal might conceivably block our mass, and that going forward he could ban Voice from meeting on church property and reject our charitable contributions. We were concerned enough about these possibilities to seek the help of Catholic theologians. Dozens of Catholic theologians signed a letter asserting our right to meet—a powerful affirmation of our rights as lay people.

On the day before the convention we held a press conference in which we announced two significant initiatives. The first was a report card that we would use to evaluate U.S. bishops and their performance on protecting children from abusive priests. The second was our Voice of Compassion fund, which would enable Catholics who did not want to donate to the archdiocese to contribute to our fund—which stipulated that the money would go to the needy rather than for secret settlements, lawyers' fees, or public relations. We held the conference at Faneuil Hall in Boston for its symbolism as an icon of democracy. Faneuil Hall is the historic Boston building where American colonists enunciated their "no taxation without representation" views and where, on America's first birthday, President George Washington led the national celebration. Our event was reported on the front page of the *Globe* with both an article and photograph from the press conference.

At the conference we called upon all bishops to vigorously enforce the zero-tolerance policies they had agreed to at their meeting in Dallas. We noted that this required the involvement of lay people on boards, panels, and other structures where broad perspectives are needed. We asserted that survivors should always be included as members as a matter of principle. We called upon bishops to work with civil authorities to use both church and civil law procedures to tighten up the system in order to protect children from sexual predators.

That night, several hundred people arrived in town for the convention. Some came by car; others by bus, train, or airplane. They came from New York and California, Chicago and Florida, Texas and Pennsylvania. They came, as well, from Mexico and Canada, from Ireland and England, and beyond.

There was really only one question that remained to be answered by our convention: Were there enough committed Catholics willing to join together and force the hierarchy to fulfill its moral duty and allow the laity to play a meaningful role in running the church? We knew we were under a microscope. We knew that the national press were watching, that bishops throughout the country and even the world were watching; we knew that Cardinal Law was watching. And we knew that in Rome, the Vatican was watching as well.

The John B. Hynes Convention Center, named for one of the city's visionary mayors, sits on Boylston Street in Boston's Back Bay neighborhood, next to the Prudential Center and its fifty-two-story tower looming over the city. On Friday night, members of Voice, out-of-town visitors, and some of our convention speakers gathered for a reception in an upstairs Hynes function room.

After the reception, Paul Baier slipped away from the crowd and went downstairs into the convention hall itself. It was deathly still, and he was struck by the vastness of it, by the sheer enormity of the room. He looked out over row upon row of perfectly aligned seats, gazed up into the balcony that seemed to go on for hundreds and hundreds of feet—and though he now knew we would, he could still hardly believe that we were about to pull it off. While hundreds of volunteers had worked hard to help make the convention a reality, the man to whom we owed the greatest debt was Paul. He was inspired—driven might be a better word—to make the church a better place.

Paul had grown up in Louisville, Ohio, where he'd gone to Catholic schools from grades one through twelve. His senior year in high school, before heading off to Kenyon College in Gambier, Ohio, Paul felt there was something he needed to get off his chest. He was sick of all the rules and rituals of Catholicism, "tired of the unending tide of guilt." He had had enough of an institution where he was not taught to understand the teachings, to really grasp them, but rather required by rote to follow along. Paul saw that Catholic ritual was rich with symbolism, but he had not been taught what the symbols meant, what deeper meanings they conveyed.

"As a young person I was told to recite these certain readings and sayings, dip my hand in holy water before and after church, bow my head when the priest came around with incense or holy water. The mass and Catholic tradition are full of symbols: the Stations of the Cross, Christ on the cross, washing of the hands, the meaning of colors, incense, ashes, music, three small crosses on body before gospel, kneeling at certain times at mass. While I am sure I was told perhaps once or twice a superficial meaning of these acts, this was not the emphasis of my Catholic education. Compliance was stressed much more than understanding. Obedience was important—I still can't figure out why *that's* a virtue," he said.

As a high school senior, Paul sought out Father Pat Manning, the younger of his school priests. Paul was direct: He told Father Pat that his plan was to avoid going to church for all four years of college. He expected Father Pat to berate him, but he could handle that for he also knew that he would have a "clean heart" because he was being truthful.

But Father Pat didn't berate him. He listened to Paul and then replied, "That's okay. But don't forget us."

Paul was taken aback—in part by the young priest's understanding of him, but also by the urging: *Don't forget us.*

And so he was done with the church—at least for a time. He departed feeling that the "only people left were nonrebels, people who need comfort, who need to follow."

What was to be a four-year hiatus from church stretched to eighteen years. Paul Baier graduated from Kenyon College and worked for the Deloitte Touche consulting firm, first in Cleveland, then Tokyo. He then went off to Harvard Business School, graduating in 1994, riding the dot-com wave up and then back down.

Everything changed for Paul when his daughter Rachel was born in 1999. Though Paul had been away from the church for many years, he knew he wanted Rachel to have faith. He needed to decide whether he was going to raise her as a Catholic; whether he, himself, was to return to Catholicism. He invested some time in study, in thinking, in talking with other people, and decided to return to his church. "I wanted to stay Catholic, to bring the teachings of Jesus to Rachel," he said.

Paul found what he wanted for Rachel at St. John's. Going to the children's mass, sitting in the front row, Paul thought "it felt right."

Ironically, around the time that the *Globe* published revelations of the sex abuse scandal and cover-up, Paul was reading about Aristotelian virtues, particularly about the cardinal virtues of courage and justice. He was stunned by the chasm between the virtues defined by Aristotle and the behavior of church leaders. "I couldn't believe the ineptness. I always thought Cardinal Law was an esteemed individual. I thought, I don't want to leave the church again. I don't want to be bullied out."

<h1 style="text-align:center">—III—</h1>

Starting around 7:30 the next morning, people began streaming through the Hynes entranceway on Boylston Street and riding the escalators up to the convention level. At first there were dozens; then scores; and then the lobby was filled with hundreds and hundreds of people, registering, chatting, greeting one another. People who had communicated by phone or e-mail were meeting for the first time. Others who had not seen one another in a while were getting reacquainted. They were middle-aged and older for the most part, with an encouraging sprinkling of younger people. It was a crowd dressed comfortably for the summer Saturday: casual skirts and pants, short-sleeved shirts, and sensible shoes.

We believed that first impressions would be lasting, and it was therefore important what first greeted our convention-goers. Mary Scanlon had had an idea about this. She had worked with survivors to understand their experience and to learn what Voice could do to acknowledge their dignity and to offer support. One of the things she learned along the way was the passionate desire of survivors to be embraced by other Catholics. And so Mary had suggested that we write an open letter to survivors and post it on our Web site. We would then invite Voice members to download the letter, then write their own personal thoughts and reflections on the letters that they had downloaded and mail them to us. Mary set aside a huge wall in the lobby of the Hynes for displaying the letters. As crowds surged through the lobby, countless people stopped and read the letters on the wall, many of them openly weeping. The letter from our group read:

> Dear Survivors,
>
> This letter is meant to convey our unconditional support to you and your families as you advance in your personal healing journey. We are inspired by your courage. We are deeply grateful for your generosity despite your profound personal loss as you reach out, not only to each other, but to us all. You help us to understand your experience and assist us in facing the sorrow, anger, and shame that has become our experience in the Church.
>
> We express our deep remorse at the mental and physical violation you have suffered. We know that words cannot erase the injury and insult to your

human dignity. We are outraged at the betrayal by those who lead the Church, especially those designated to care for our young. We are filled with shame at the inadequacy of our Church's apologetic response to the offenses against you.

We are sorry if our silence has increased your pain and suffering. We are sorry for our ignorance, our failing to act in a timely manner on accumulating evidence of widespread abuse, and our perceived willingness to believe that particular incidents of sexual abuse were exceptions. We know that whether innocent child, youth, or vulnerable adult, you were defenseless in the face of a powerful person and institution. We attest that the abuse of children by priests and the cover-up by Church leadership are not only sinful acts but also criminal offenses.

To you, the survivors of sexual abuse by priests, we pledge:

To listen to you.

To seek ways to help you.

To support recovery services for you and your families.

To advocate for criminal prosecution for the perpetrators of abuse and those who obstructed justice in the pursuit of these crimes.

To work for reform of civil laws and Church institutions that have contributed to the offenses against you.

Not to interfere with your spiritual journey, but to nurture your individual quest as you seek solace.

In all these things, we stand in solidarity with you.

Standing on the vast stage in front of the packed auditorium, Susan Troy began our day with prayer and by standing "in solidarity" with our "brothers and sisters who have suffered abuse from Catholic priests." We spent the opening fifteen minutes in prayer led by Susan, Svea, and Sister Betsy Conway, C.S.J. Susan gave a heartfelt welcome to "those who have been abused in your suffering, in your pain, in your courage to speak the truth, you have brought us to this place . . . we honor you and we thank you."

Jim Post, who had recently been elected our new president while I remained chairman, greeted the crowd with great enthusiasm, noting that gathered together at the Hynes were more than four thousand people from thirty states and eight foreign nations. And then Jim introduced me as a "visionary" for my role in founding Voice of the Faithful.

As I stepped up to the podium, I thought back to our first meeting in the basement of St. John's Church with several dozen parishioners. Now, a matter of months later, I was looking out over an international convention being reported to the world by the media.

"It is an honor and a joy to address this holy gathering of Catholics—this magnificent response of the faithful," I said. "As I suspect is true for many of you, there was a time just months ago when I could take no joy in contemplation of our church, when I could barely attend mass. The revelations of massive sexual abuse by clergy and the pervasive cover-ups awakened me to the terrible flaws in our church. I reached the painful conclusion that I must either attempt to correct these deep structural defects or leave the Catholic Church."

I observed that too much unchecked power was concentrated in the hands of the hierarchy. I argued in favor of a partnership between laity and church leaders that I believed would strengthen the institution.

I concluded my remarks by projecting a color slide of a magnificent 750-year-old Catalan Gothic cathedral that Kathleen and I had visited in Majorca just two weeks earlier. "This cathedral," I noted, "resulted from a collaboration between the hierarchy, which planned the project, and thousands of laity who provided the funding and lifted the stones, over the course of hundreds of years. May the appreciation of divinity that this structure invites inspire us in our task ahead—of keeping the faith and building a new, stronger, deeply moral, modern, ancient, and holy Catholic Church, buttressed by our efforts and our prayers."

— IV —

Back when we were considering who our keynote speaker should be, one of our members, Carolyn Disco of Merrimack, New Hampshire, suggested that we should select a priest and award him a Voice of the Faithful Priest of Integrity Award. Carolyn then offered the name of Rev. Thomas Doyle, one of the authors of the Vatican-sponsored Doyle-Mouton report from 1985 concerning the breadth and significance of the sexual abuse problem among priests.

Tom Doyle was a brilliant young rising star in the Catholic hierarchy back in the 1970s and 1980s. He held a prominent position in the Vatican embassy in Washington, where he lived the vaunted life of a diplomat. In the early 1980s, word reached Father Doyle that a priest in Louisiana had been charged with molesting dozens of children. Apparently the local bishop there had shuffled the offender from one location to the next. As he investigated, Father Doyle was shocked to learn that it wasn't just one priest but in fact numerous priests who had been sexually abusing children. He had believed at the time that the Catholic hierarchy—when presented with the facts—would do what was right.

Father Doyle's work led the Vatican to send Bishop A. J. Quinn of Cleveland to Louisiana to investigate more deeply. Working with one of the lawyers in Louisiana, Father Doyle put together a report for Bishop Quinn indicating that the problem of sexual abuse by priests was significant and extended throughout the country. Father Doyle predicted that the problem could potentially cost the church one *billion* dollars in legal settlements. This was in 1985.

A committee was formed but Father Doyle would subsequently learn that it was little more than a PR move by the church. Father Doyle was relentless in his pursuit of truth about the issue; so relentless that it became uncomfortable for the hierarchy, which clearly wanted the issue kept as quiet as possible. Because of his persistence, Father Doyle was dismissed from his position at the Vatican embassy and assigned to work in Greenland. By the late 1990s he had become a U.S. Air Force chaplain at the Ramstein Air Base in Germany. But through all the years his avocation had become unceasing work to counsel and support victims as well as to call attention to the seriousness of the sexual abuse problem within the church. For hundreds of victims/survivors, he had become an iconic figure. We decided he was the perfect person to receive our Priest of Integrity Award *and* to deliver our keynote address.

Father Doyle arrived in town the night before the convention and met with old friends with whom he had worked on survivor issues. For so many years prior to the *Globe*'s revelations, the survivor community attracted so little attention or support from other Catholics that Father Doyle was, as he later put it, "blown away" by the size of the convention and the breadth of topics to be covered.

"The people I met the first night were about the most impressive group of Catholics I had ever met," said Father Doyle. "Decent, good, upbeat, insightful—filled with hope and faith and above all, justifiably angry at what their church leaders had done." Throughout the evening before—and throughout Saturday—Father Doyle was being interviewed by the media "almost constantly. I was simply shocked at all the attention they were giving me."

Father Doyle had arrived in Boston without a prepared speech, so he stayed up Friday night until two o'clock in the morning, writing. He rose just four hours later at 6 A.M. and continued to work on the speech.

"When I walked into the packed auditorium and stood there as Jim read the citation for the award, I was stunned. Nothing like that had ever happened to me and it was something I never expected. I got very fired up from the initial response of the audience, and when they kept applauding it only fired me up more, so I let loose."

In introducing Father Doyle, Jim Post said that Father Doyle had incurred the wrath of the hierarchy and been accused of being "a loose cannon and a time bomb."

Amid loud applause, Father Doyle took the stage, went to the microphone, and loudly proclaimed "I'm still a loose cannon and a time bomb!" causing the applause to grow even louder. Thomas Doyle was fifty-seven years old, a fit, square-jawed man with the robust appearance of an athlete. He stood tall and gazed out over the gathering, clearly thrilled to be there, and he spoke in a powerful, exuberant voice.

> I would not be here were it not for the goodness, courage, and faith of the many, many victims and survivors whom I have met over the many years that we have been chasing the demon of clergy sexual abuse. The horrendous physical and spiritual damage they have suffered and the courage and fighting spirit that has prompted them to forge ahead has inspired me. . . .
>
> [M]y commitment continues to be vivified by that of the victims and survivors who are, in truth, the most important people in God's church because they are the ones Christ Himself would be sitting with today.

This was so plain and clear, so obvious to all of us, that we were at a loss to explain why the bishops did not grasp this eloquent thought. There was a popular bracelet that many people wore around this time with the initials WWJD—What would Jesus do? The expression was a way of helping people make good decisions, guiding them to live in the image of Jesus Christ. It was so clear what Jesus would do in this case: Of course He would seek out the victims and survivors to give comfort and care!

Father Doyle generously acknowledged many of his friends and colleagues. At one point he acknowledged the work of the press in uncovering the truth about sexual abuse by priests, singling out "the revolutionary continuing exposé of the *Boston Globe*." At this, the people rose and cheered—the first time I had ever witnessed a standing ovation for a newspaper! Then he continued:

> The despicable saga of clergy and religious sexual abuse is not the essence of the problem. It is a symptom of a deeper, much more pervasive and destructive disease that is nearly fatal in nature: *the fallacy of clericalism.*
>
> The primary symptom of this virus is the delusion that the clergy are somehow above the laity, deserving of unquestioned privilege and stature, the keepers of our salvation and the guarantors of our favor with the Lord. *The deadliest symptom, however, is the unbridled addiction to power . . .*
>
> This widespread and deeply ingrained abuse of power by the hierarchical leadership of our church has been sustained and even encouraged by the myth that what is good for that tiny minority, the clergy, is identified with what is good for the church. The church, according to this erroneous way of thinking, is the clergy and the hierarchy. But they have lost sight of the Christ-given reality that

the church is *us*. Its most vital and important members are not those who wear the elaborate robes and sit on the thrones of power, but the marginalized, the hurting, the rejected and the abused.

What we see happening around us are the initial death throes of the medieval monarchical model of the church. This was and is an institutional church that was based on the belief that a small, select minority of the educated, the privileged and the powerful was called by Almighty God to manage the temporal and spiritual lives of the faceless masses, on the presumption that their unlettered and squalid state meant that they were ignorant and incapable of discerning their spiritual destiny. This is 2002 and not 1302, and that model is based on a myth that is long dead, if in fact it was ever remotely grounded in a sliver of reality. . . .

We are often told that this model is based on God's will, grounded in an interpretation of Christ's action in giving the "Keys to the Kingdom" to St. Peter. Rather than depend totally on this statement as the rationale for the hierarchical system which was later invested with all of the trappings of monarchy, there is another statement of Christ that is a more accurate reflection of His vision for human government. We find it in Mark's Gospel:

You know that in the world the recognized rulers lord it over their subjects, and their great men make them feel the weight of authority. This is not the way with you; among you, whoever wants to be great must be your servant, and whoever wants to be the first must be the willing slave of all. [Mark 10: 42–43]

. . . If we listen to the words of Christ and especially learn from his actions, we see looming up that word that strikes fear and trembling in churchmen. . . . *democracy!* Why? Because it surely is evident that this was the reality that Christ lived by in his ministry. . . .

This terrible disaster that we are living through has proven beyond any doubt the need for all Catholics and indeed all Christians to abandon the magical thinking about the hierarchy and clergy that sustains the medieval paradigm. We must accept the great risk involved in accepting Christ's challenge *to lead by serving.* The hierarchical system appears to have lost its ability to do this . . .

We live in the hope that we will see a church that is a Christ-centered community of equal believers first, and a political structure second. This hope is within our grasp and within our vision.

There is no longer any justification for timidity and deference to the very structures and leaders who have betrayed us. Our church has been hijacked and we want it back!

We must challenge any deacon, priest, or bishop who voices his support for the victims and survivors and who hopes for a re-vivified church to not simply talk, but act!

We must keep this wonderful, hopeful spirit alive. The pope, the cardinals, and the bishops, and indeed millions have been praying for relief from this crisis . . . praying for a new dawn. We believe that our prayers are being answered and the new dawn is breaking and a sure sign of it is here today. The Spirit of God is really alive and well and staying involved! It is here and it is moving through all of you . . .

For years this sex abuse nightmare has caused so many of us to question everything we knew and believed about our church and even to wonder if the Lord cared. Being here this weekend, bound up in faith and hope with the survivors and with all of you, has been for me and for so many, an indescribable moment. God is alive and thriving in His church and you are the proof. Your response to the victims, to the survivors and indeed to the whole Catholic community as we painfully live through this tragedy, is a response to God's promptings. It is the most eloquent and convincing proof that our Lord is with us and, *He Cares.*

The applause was thunderous. We stood—all 4,200 of us—and roared our approval, cheered our heroic priest of integrity. And in that speech—in that electrifying moment when we all rose as one and applauded this wonderful man—our convention was transformed, and so too were we. Rarely had I heard a presentation so urgent, so powerful, so right! I believe there was divine inspiration, that the Holy Spirit was present with us in the Hynes Auditorium. For the remainder of the day it was as though two enormously powerful currents had merged, joining together to lift us and propel us forward. One current was the glow of the speech by Father Doyle; the other was divine inspiration.

—⚉—

The speakers who came after Tom Doyle had a near-impossible task, but the truth is they were all good. Each speaker added something important and insightful to the day. Steve Pope of Boston College took the stage and said in his steady, measured voice that the bishops had to be held accountable for their negligence and deception. He said that there was not only a right among the laity to speak out on important issues but an obligation as well. To rousing applause, Steve said that no longer should sheep be the symbol of laity in the Catholic Church. "Many Catholics have to get over the idea that the mission of the laity is to clean up the deck chairs after the parish picnic."

Peggie Thorp then said that she had wondered whether our church could "survive another day under the weight of its own culture," but she said that this day proved "the voice of the laity will never again be silenced."

As one of the leading Jesuit universities in the world, Boston College played a crucial role in the religious and civic life of Greater Boston, and its faculty was well represented at our conference. In addition to Steve Pope there were other speakers from BC. Lisa Sowle Cahill, a BC theologian, contrasted church reform in the wake of Vatican II and in the wake of the sex abuse scandal. The result of Vatican II, she said, was reform from the top down—mandated by the pope and bishops. This time, she said, reform was being pushed from the bottom up. BC theologian Thomas Groome said that God would surely work through an awakened laity. He strongly echoed Father Doyle's belief that it was essential to "break down" the notion of clericalism—the idea that that priests and bishops were somehow higher or better or closer to God. Clericalism, he said, creates conditions conducive to pedophilia and cover-up, and it must be eradicated. Dr. Francine Cardman from the faculty of the Weston Jesuit School of Theology was inspirational.

Jim Post spoke eloquently about our movement being one that included a broad range of Catholics—survivors and their parents and siblings, "women religious, whose voices have too often not been heard, priests, men and women who have been away from the church, people who celebrate Vatican II, and people who want to celebrate the Latin mass.

"Our job," Jim said, "is to rebuild what others have damaged." Jim said that we wanted our bishops to be open to us, to talk with us, to listen to us. But he made clear that we would not be talked down to or silenced: "We will not negotiate our right to exist; we will not negotiate our right to be heard," he said to a loud ovation.

— V —

In the late afternoon, toward the end of the convention, a section of the program had been set dedicated to survivors. Mary Scanlon had worked hard to make sure we had the right lineup. She had chosen three people: Phil Saviano, who had spoken so eloquently at one of our Monday night meetings; Pat Serrano, the mother of a sex abuse victim from New Jersey; and Barbara Blaine, who had been sexually abused by a priest and founded the national group SNAP, or Survivors Network of those Abused by Priests. David Clohessy, the executive director of SNAP, had also joined us.

But just one week before the convention, Mary attended a meeting of the group Coalition of Catholics and Survivors, and members told her that they thought Voice was not focused sufficiently on survivor issues. At one point, a man named Arthur Austin, a well-known survivor activist, said of Voice: "You say you are willing to support survivors but you won't stand beside us because you think we're dirty."

Mary was stunned by this. She felt we had made a genuine effort to support survivors and she was taken aback that Arthur would harbor such a belief. But Mary's approach was to listen to survivors, to try and understand them—to honor them and to do whatever she could to demonstrate support for them. And so, although the program for the convention was as close to being set in stone as possible, Mary felt that it was imperative that we hear Arthur's message, however harsh. On the Wednesday night prior to the convention, there was a planning committee conference call during which Mary made a passionate plea to have Arthur invited as a speaker. After intense discussion, it was agreed that Arthur Austin would be added. Still, the convention was picketed by a small number of survivors who felt we had not done enough to support them.

Now, in the late afternoon, just before mass was to be celebrated, Phil Saviano stood before us, a broad smile on his face as he held up a poster-sized photograph of a little boy—Phil at age twelve, when he was first abused. The trauma, he said, had separated him from the church. He described himself as a "spiritual drifter" who "never made it back to shore."

He looked out over the capacity crowd—out over the 4,200 people of faith—and he spoke with a wistful tone of envy. "All of my life I have seen people like yourselves gain peace, strength, and fulfillment in rituals of the Catholic Church. I can't imagine what that's like."

It was a breathtaking moment. *I can't imagine what that's like.* We were all here because of the power of our faith, thousands of us, and here was Phil, whose experience had been so hellish that he had lost his. It was a brutal moment for many of us—for me, the most sorrowful moment of the convention.

Pat Serrano, the mother of a boy who had been molested as a child, spoke movingly. She recalled that when her son finally went to a bishop to report what had happened, the bishop had urged him not to tell his parents—because it might upset them.

Barbara Blaine, the national founder of SNAP, talked about having been molested by a priest for four and a half years—starting when she was just thirteen.

"I *couldn't* tell anyone," she said. "I *didn't* tell anyone."

And then came Arthur Austin. He was in his late forties, tall, blond, balding, with piercing eyes. Mary introduced Arthur and he stepped to the podium. He stood quite still and spoke in a low, steady voice with little inflection. There was an intensity to his tone, and his words were unflinching.

> Good afternoon. Thank you for this opportunity to speak to you. I want to address the issue of the angry survivors outside who want nothing to do with you. For them, quite legitimately, your

splendid conference is too little, too late, and too much about you, when it should always and urgently, and long since, have been about them. For them, this event is a shadow-play, a thing without substance. And before you begin to grow indignant with me for saying this, let me ask you—how many of you took the time even to find out the name of one of those angry survivors? . . .

You have never walked one step, one moment, of their agonizing, lonely, and hellishly terrifying journey. You do not live in a perpetually catastrophic moment. They do. So do I. You do not get to judge them, all you get is the right to beg their forgiveness . . .

The time has come when Voice of the Faithful must make a . . . choice between its desire for merely public and churchly respectability before all else, or the extremely unmanageable, unpredictable, and often alarming, radical grace of God in the world.

There are 4,200 of you here today, to honor your highly strategized, thoroughly debated and very, very quiet agenda; and yet on Sunday, June 23rd, at the Solidarity Walk to honor the humanity and courage of the priest-abused, both living and dead, your presence was noticeable only by its vast invisibility. The presence of your absence was everywhere.

After prayer and reflection, I have been moved to ask you two questions today, in the name of every victim we remembered on that Sunday, including myself. First: Where *were* you on Sunday, the 23rd of June 2002, as the dead were honored and the living comforted in the shadow of the very church that had harmed them? And second, the simple, but fatigued and heartbroken question of Gethsemane: "What, could you not keep watch even one hour with me?"

In God's name I challenge the members of Voice of the Faithful, after their liturgy, to walk from this convention hall, with me, to the Cathedral of the Holy Cross to stand in solidarity with each survivor victim who trusts you enough to let you walk with them. . . .

I invite my fellow-survivors, who know what it means to suffer, who have spent decades healing themselves, to walk with me, to reach out in their hard-won and unique wisdom and profound capacity for personal compassion, to people who are barely groping their way toward understanding, and let the healing begin.

Thank you for your attention. May Almighty

God bless you, and may each of you go in the peace
and love of your church, which the victims of that
church *no longer know* . . .

Many people in the hall were shocked by Arthur's words.
Some were moved, others angered, yet Arthur was received with
sustained applause. On stage, Mary Scanlon embraced Arthur
when he was finished speaking. She walked with him down off
the stage past the Voice of the Faithful Steering Committee and
she burst into tears. She worried that her friends in our group
considered Arthur's speech an insult—and some did. Some believed that his behavior had been rude and unnecessary—that
we had been working as hard as humanly possible to try and
make the church a better, safer place for survivors. But most of
us also tried hard to understand. We wanted to understand the
world as Arthur and other survivors saw it, and his speech had
certainly helped us do that.

The stage was being set up for mass and Mary was walking
with Arthur, escorting him out to the lobby. But as they were
walking out Arthur stopped and turned to Mary. He told her he
wanted to stay for mass. He had not been to mass in decades, but
now, he told her, he wanted to stay. And he did so, standing off
to the side, Mary holding his hand throughout as Arthur wept.

Father William Kremmell, the chaplain at Regis and Framingham State Colleges, embraced the crowd with his blessing at
the beginning of mass. He elicited laughter from the audience

when he said that twenty-five years ago such a gathering of Catholics would surely have sought to get the bishop to celebrate mass for them. Father Kremmell—in a daring statement—said he hoped that in another twenty-five years a married woman might be celebrating such a mass. While the reading of the Gospel is generally reserved for priests only, Father Kremmell invited lay men and women to join with him in the readings.

When it came time for the Eucharist, Mary shared her communion with Arthur. And when the mass was over, Arthur and Mary headed out of the hall and down on to Boylston Street for their walk to the Cathedral of the Holy Cross. Would a dozen people follow? Mary wondered. A hundred? Would *anyone*?

As they were going out, Jimmy Breslin, the writer, approached Arthur. He said that he and his wife wanted to accompany Arthur to the cathedral but they were unable to walk such a distance. Would it be all right, Breslin asked, if they took a cab and met them there?

And then the procession began down Boylston on a gorgeous summer night, the air warm and comforting. After a block or so, Mary dared to turn around and look back. What she saw made her heart soar. There they were, the Catholics who had journeyed to Boston for the convention—hundreds and hundreds of men and women walking solemnly in procession, responding to Arthur Austin's challenge to walk to the cathedral and stand at the side of survivors. The walk was somehow transcendent, the evening so blessed and beautiful. When the procession arrived at the cathedral, there was Jimmy Breslin, waiting. The throng spontaneously gathered around Arthur Austin. Someone urged him to say something. Arthur was uncharacteristically at a loss for words. After a moment of silence, he smiled and said, "I guess what I want to say"—and here he thrust his arms into the air as though embracing the entire crowd—"is *thank you!*"

—⟶⟨⟨⟨⟶—

If that's where it had ended, there would have been a sort of storybook quality to the Arthur Austin story; but it actually got better the following day. Mass the next morning at the cathedral—as was tradition—was celebrated by Cardinal Law. Mary and others from our group accompanied Arthur to the cathedral that morning because they wanted again to show their support. When time came for the Eucharist, a moment of considerable drama began to play out. Arthur Austin—who was usually outside the cathedral protesting—was now inside and he was in the line filing toward the altar rail where the Cardinal was giving out communion. Austin had spoken out against Bernard Law in public for a long time and in brutal terms. What would happen? Would the Cardinal's security detail intercept him as they had others, to keep him away from Law? Would Arthur get close to the Cardinal and berate him? Insult him? Or worse?

No. Arthur received communion from Cardinal Law. And as he did so, Arthur said to the Cardinal, "Please pray for me."

As Arthur turned away to return to his pew, Law reached out and grasped Arthur firmly by the upper arm and said to Arthur, "I will. And please pray for me."

Svea was moved by what she felt was a compassionate gesture by the Cardinal. The next morning she picked up the phone and called the chancery. She didn't reach Law directly, but she got his voice mail. She felt that she had been critical of the Cardinal—and appropriately so—and that now he had done something that had moved her and she wanted him to know it. She left a message commending him for his response to Arthur, saying that both of their gestures "had touched all of us."

— VI —

On Sunday morning, the day after the convention, the *Globe's* front-page headline read, "LAY CATHOLICS ISSUE CALL TO TRANSFORM THEIR CHURCH." The article, by Michael Paulson, began:

> Taking direct aim at the millennia-old power structure of the world's largest religious denomination, some four thousand Roman Catholics from across the United States gathered in Boston yesterday and

vowed to transform a church that they say betrayed them by failing to protect children from sexual abuse.

The members of Voice of the Faithful, a lay reform group born in a church basement in Wellesley just five months ago, used the occasion of their first national convention to begin flexing their collective muscle.

Paulson quoted me as saying, "The core of the problem is centralized power, with no voice of the faithful. The people of Boston know what to do about absolute power—they showed the world 200 years ago."

Father Tom Doyle left the convention believing that Voice of the Faithful was "a gift from the Holy Spirit." He said he considered our group "the single most hopeful sign of growth for the Catholic Church. It is a sign that the lay people are finally emerging from their childlike status into full adulthood. This will have a profound impact."

As a movement, Voice of the Faithful emerged from the convention significantly empowered. With positive worldwide publicity, we had been established as a force to be reckoned with. By anyone's measure, it was genuinely remarkable: In just a few short months, our movement had grown from a gathering in a church basement to a force for democracy within the Roman Catholic Church.

CHAPTER 9

THE HISTORICAL CASE FOR A DEMOCRACY OF THE LAITY

— I —

THE CONTRAST BETWEEN the spirit of democracy flourishing at the convention and the autocratic disdain I had witnessed at the chancery led me to realize that two massive forces were moving toward an historic encounter. The grassroots democracy that had arisen from the people of Boston was now engaging a monarchical system that, despite great success in the advocacy of the teachings of Christ over the centuries, had again revealed its structural flaws.

The magnitude of these forces and the importance of the outcome of the encounter were clear enough, but many of us were not well versed in the issues to be joined. In particular, we did not know enough about the history of democratic practices within our two-thousand-year-old church. We were fortunate to have a number of individuals such as Svea Fraser and Susan Troy who had studied church history.

We learned that the Catholic Church, particularly since Vatican II, defines itself as the People of God, a pilgrim church on earth that moves through history on its way toward the final kingdom of God. The second chapter of the Dogmatic Constitution on the Church (*Lumen Gentium*) is entitled "The People of God." *The Documents of Vatican II*, edited by Walter M. Abbott, S. J. state: "This title (THE PEOPLE OF GOD), solidly founded in Scripture, met a profound desire of the Council to put greater emphasis on the human and communal side of the Church, rather than the institutional and hierarchical aspects which have sometimes been overstressed in the past. While everything said about the People of God as a whole is applicable to the laity, it should not be forgotten that the term 'People of God' refers to the total community of the Church, including the pastors as well as the other faithful."

Svea noted that the pilgrim church is one that adapts some of its practices based on its movement through history, in which *praxis*, or reflective action, is part of the process. We in Voice believe that this process would be facilitated by the input of the collective wisdom of the laity, the *sensus fidelium*.

In an optimal civil democracy, the will of the people should be primary—it is the foundation for the legitimacy of the government. The church, in contrast, consists of a core doctrine, which is accepted by the faithful without debate. However, this core doctrine is surrounded by many other issues in which the will of the people should play a far stronger role than it currently does.

To my surprise, I also learned that as laity we were not just "ordinary people" in a system dominated by clergy, but also "priests" in our own right. Svea quoted Chapter IV of the Constitution on the Church, which states that lay people are "by baptism made one body with Christ and are constituted the People of God and in their own way made sharers in the priestly, prophetical and kingly functions of Christ." The document continues, "Though they differ from one another in essence and not only in degree, the common priesthood of the faithful and the ministerial or hierarchical priesthood are nonetheless interrelated. Each of them in its own special way is a participation in the one priesthood of Christ." This added legitimacy to our efforts to discern and assert our collective thoughts.

To me, the concepts of the priestly role of the laity and the *sensus fidelium* were in some ways parallel to the concept in a civil democracy that leadership should arise from the people who were "endowed with certain inalienable rights," as stated in the Declaration of Independence. Father Tom had reinforced this idea in our first meeting when he said, with a quiet voice, "you *are* the Church," expressing the radical idea of the New Testament, reinforced by Vatican II, and alive in our church basement.

Father Tom added that of course Catholic dialogue must take into account a specific faith tradition—it must recognize a Catholic identity. We would later invite the author Michele Dillon to discuss her book *A Catholic Identity* in which the limits of democratic self-direction by groups of Catholics are discussed.

As far back as our initial meeting, my wife, Kathleen, stated that we needed to learn more about the current structure of the church, whose mysteries were not limited to the spiritual domain. The hierarchy was full of administrators, personnel policies, budgets, and lawyers working in a manner that had produced such good, and now, we learned, such evil. How did it work?

Svea, who opened many paths to knowledge for us, suggested that we all read *The Changing Face of the Priesthood* by Father Donald Cozzens. I added this to my reading, which would soon include more than thirty books on the church. Father Cozzens wrote from his perspective as an insider. He was president-rector and professor of pastoral theology at Saint Mary Seminary and Graduate School of Theology in Cleveland, Ohio, and he had the courage to write about the bad, as well as the good, that his position as a teacher of priests permitted him to view.

His book was published two years before the *Boston Globe* broke the story of the current scandal, and yet the sexual abuse of children by priests, and the failure of the hierarchy to deal with the problem, were fully presented and analyzed. He noted that clergy misconduct with minors, which is likely to have existed throughout church history, was first considered a "crisis" in the mid-1980s in the United States. He participated in meetings with church leaders where the problem was addressed. "I recall no thoughtful discussions about the causes of the problem, its meaning or implications. Attempts to do so were often met with a suspicion that a certain agenda was at work," he writes.

He went on to note that the Vatican cast as dissenters bishops and others who sought to discuss topics such as married priests and women's ordination, which some thought might help prevent such scandal in the future. He wrote of the great disillusionment that accompanied the failure of the institutional church to fully implement the opening up of the church that Vatican II had envisioned. He noted that there had even been a relapse into preconciliar practices in some areas. But in his conclusion he noted that a sign of hope was the awakening of the laity, "who see the Spirit at work in the People of God."

Eighteen months later I received a handwritten letter from Donald Cozzens, whom I had never met, in which he wrote, "Your leadership role, and that of Jim Post, in Voice, is a great grace for our Church. I truly believe it is the laity's moment." Later, Svea and Scott hosted a dinner for Kathleen and me to meet Donald. I brought his book and showed him the underlined portions that had been part of the intellectual capital that contributed to the formation of Voice. Svea then brought out her copy, in which we found she had underlined the same thoughts.

— I I —

As newcomers to the issue of church structure, we had first sought out experts on canon law. But we also knew we needed to hear some novel and thus controversial views, since it was apparent that the current structure was not working properly.

I called Father Richard McBrien, a brilliant scholar of Catholic history and church structure who had served as the chair of the theology department of the University of Notre Dame. In the dark days of January 2002, I had heard Father McBrien speak many times on national television. His comments reminded me why I had taken such pride in Catholicism and attending Notre Dame.

Back then I had explained to Father McBrien that we had a small group in a parish near Boston that wanted to change the church in light of the sex abuse scandal (at the time we had about sixty members). I told him we had concluded that the underlying problem was the concentration of power in the hierarchy. Father McBrien treated this rather simplistic formulation of a problem he had spent years studying with great respect. "Yes," he said, "you are right."

"The problem," he observed, "is that the legislative, executive, and judicial powers of the Catholic Church are all in the hands of the hierarchy." I reported his thoughts back to the group, who incorporated this idea into our prescription for change.

I also called Professor Scott Appleby, the director of the Cushwa Center for the Study of American Catholicism at Notre Dame, whom I had also heard commenting on the scandal. As with Father McBrien, I introduced myself as a Notre Dame alumnus and described our small group and our outsized intentions. While he admired our goal of changing the church, Scott, with his extensive knowledge of church history, told me he didn't think we had much of a chance. But then, after a pause in which I tried to maintain my enthusiasm for the task, he came back with a possibility.

"No," he said, "let me take that back. You might succeed if the laity could organize their financial power. You would need to be able to influence the flow of money."

This emphasis on financial power certainly fit well with my limited experience of church politics. In the 1970s the wealthy parishioners in Indianapolis had forced the local bishop to re-instate my uncle, whom he had fired as pastor. I reported Scott's advice about the money back to the group. Jim Post, David Castaldi, Joe and Lynn Finn, and others with experience in financial matters then created the Voice of Compassion Fund—a fund dedicated to support of the sick and needy—that would provide such financial power for the laity.

During the same conversation, perhaps emboldened by his vision of financial power as a tool of change, Scott joined our spirit of considering the unlikely—but not impossible—prospect that the church could be changed by the laity. He began to give advice about democratic structures in Catholicism.

"The early American Church had quite a bit of democracy," he added. "You should read about Bishop John England of South Carolina in the early 1800s. He established a bicameral legislature of clergy and laity to help run the diocese." And like a chess master thinking several moves ahead, Scott added, "But if you get into advocating that, you will be accused by the Vatican of the error of 'Americanism.'"

The mention of the Vatican reminded me of something Peggie Thorp had said when we first spoke of the shocking revelations in St. John's church; she believed the problem extended all the way to Rome. While this is a reasonable conclusion in a church that stresses its unity and the primacy of the pope, it is difficult to believe that someone with the many strengths of John Paul II would tolerate such behavior. Now, Scott's comments reinforced my sense that the governance of the church was far more complex than I had appreciated. We needed a better understanding of church structure, including that of the papacy.

—III—

John Paul II has elevated the stature of the papacy. He has been a prominent advocate for the impoverished, for improved interfaith dialogue, for freedom in the face of totalitarian regimes, and much more. He has provided an inspiring example of the teaching of Christ by forgiving the man who shot him, and over the years he has won the admiration of many young Catholics. On a personal level, he has been a model of holiness for me, and of course I will never forget the direct assistance he provided with his letter supporting our work for the prevention of nuclear war.

At the same time, this pope, and many in the Curia (the senior administrators of the hierarchy) currently holding Vatican leadership positions under the pope's authority, have sought to reestablish administrative practices and central control that many consider to be a reversal of the changes created by Vatican II. For example, consideration of an expanded role for women in the church have been limited and further discussion about the possibility of ordination of women to the priesthood has been forbidden by papal decree. Priests who might become bishops have been required to state their allegiance to current teachings of the church that extend far beyond the Immaculate Conception of Mary and her Assumption into Heaven, the only two proclamations that have been deemed to be infallible. And many of the bishops implicated in the current abuse crisis were selected by the current Vatican leadership for their unquestioning loyalty.

Hence, the current papacy and Curia hold great power—some derived from structure and some derived from the widespread admiration for Pope John Paul II. This power has been used in an expansive manner externally, and a consolidating manner internally. It is certainly not tempered by a worldwide lay organization of any power. While most believe, as do I, that Pope John Paul II has brought honor to the Catholic Church and the papacy, there is little protection against abuse of such absolute power by a less talented and honorable pope, as has occurred in the past and could well occur in the future. It is also possible, in a system without accountability to laity, for some surrounding the pope to abuse power.

The pope and the Curia recognize the need to rely on the power of local bishops and archbishops in the administration of their dioceses. Bishops are both appointed by the pope and autonomous leaders of their dioceses. They are not delegates, but govern in their own right within universal norms. Hence the importance to the Vatican of selecting bishops who are in agreement not only with core doctrine but also with a broad range of Vatican policies and administrative practices.

The degree to which laity share in this power of the bishops depends on the administrative style of the bishop. Most bishops hold the power closely, and few share power with clergy and laity as completely as did Bishop England. National organizations such as the United States Catholic Conference of Bishops have no direct authority over bishops—hence the group has much less power than its well-publicized meetings suggest.

Success of the local church is therefore dependent on the personal performance of the bishop, who is instructed by Vatican II teachings to form a strong partnership with the laity. The system can work extremely well with a bishop who wishes to share power with the laity. Cardinal Bernardin, with whom I had worked in the peace movement, is a prime example. But such power sharing is neither enforced nor encouraged by the Vatican. It is a system that will give free rein to a tyrant and the unchecked power can even induce poor performance by an intelligent, holy, well meaning, not previously tyrannical individual. I believe that is the tragedy that befell Cardinal Law.

Other bishops have fallen victim to this monarchical system in ways that are less sinister than the cover-up of child abuse but are still distressing. In the November 17, 2002 edition of *Newsday* I read the story of Bishop William Murphy's elegant new residence in the Rockville Centre Diocese on Long Island. The paper reported that Bishop Murphy decided he needed a better residence, so he evicted a group of nuns from a large convent and converted much of the third floor into his personal living space. He installed a gourmet kitchen with a wine closet and separate climate controls for various vintages. Dinners for twenty would be held in his dining room. The estimated cost of the renovations: $5 million. The bishop defended his efforts to build a proper home and began a continued debate with the columnist Jimmy Breslin over the propriety of the expenditures. Since the details of the project remained secret, Mr. Breslin routinely surveyed the trash behind the bishop's residence to monitor what was being purchased.

The fundamental problem that is now so obvious to many Americans is the existence of a functioning monarchy within a modern democracy. The imperial style of many in the Catholic hierarchy, exemplified by Bishop Murphy's expenditures, illustrates the flaw in the structure that permitted the cover-up of sexual abuse by so many bishops.

Among its many positive changes, the Second Vatican Council called for structures intended to soften this top-down system by actively engaging the laity in the governance and guidance (our words) of the church. The council called for, but did not require, the establishment of finance and pastoral councils at the diocesan level, and parish and finance councils at the parish level. Many devout lay people joined these councils at the invitation of the hierarchy and have made positive contributions to the church through their efforts.

However, a number of difficulties have limited the effectiveness of this Vatican II initiative. In some dioceses and parishes, the structures have not been established. Even when the structures are formed, their effectiveness is limited by their "consultative" status. In most cases, the hierarchy is free to disregard their advice.

There is also a problem in the nature of the lay representation. Since the members are, in most cases, handpicked by the hierarchy, outspoken individuals who might bring valuable, alternative points of view are not likely to be included. And in most cases members can be dismissed by the bishop or pastor for disagreeing too vehemently. The councils have been referred to by some lay Catholics as "Yes, Father, you are right" committees.

Finally, since the lay members participate in these committees as individuals, they cannot present a prioritized, consensus view of the laity, backed by discussions and debate, and legitimately represent the collective power of the laity.

—⟊—

Despite these limitations, lay committees occasionally exert considerable power. The story of the finance council of Boston is an extreme example of the power of the laity. In early 2002, in the months after the Geoghan revelations, Cardinal Law reached an agreement to pay millions of dollars to a subgroup of Geoghan's abuse survivors. The agreement was announced, and it seemed that a positive step had finally occurred. Then in a dramatic reversal it was announced that a little-known lay finance council, whose members had been appointed by Cardinal Law, had rejected the settlement. The finance council reportedly was concerned that the award of so much money to a subgroup of the survivors would exhaust the funds available for the remaining survivors and, in addition, set an average price for settlement that would bankrupt the archdiocese.

Regardless of the merits of the case, the dramatic public reversal provided a rare view of the exercise of power at a high level by the laity. While we at Voice of the Faithful were struggling to organize at the grassroots level, fearing the Cardinal might ban us from even assembling, this group of laity, many of whom had made major donations to the church, were apparently making one of the highest-level decisions possible. I admired their courage in taking such a difficult stand, and marveled at the degree of lay participation in governance being demonstrated.

Some argued that the lay finance committee was merely being used as cover by the Cardinal for his decision. While he may have welcomed their decision, we learned that the lay committee acted independently of the cardinal after Joe Finn, a co-founder of Voice, notified the committee of a canon law indicating that expenditures above a certain threshold required the committee's approval. Had the committee functioned in such a manner in the past, it is possible that the prior payments to silence abuse victims would not have been permitted.

Thus, as in seventeenth-century Europe, church governance is not absolute rule by the pope and his delegates but includes the exercise of power by a Catholic lay aristocracy, valued by the hierarchy for their donations and in some cases expertise. We realized that Voice would be most effective if it could combine the power of individuals like those who served on the diocesan finance committee and had influence with the hierarchy because of their financial and professional donations, with the power of the millions of Catholics we sought to organize who had no such influence. The combination of millions of members and millions of dollars, we believe, would provide the balance to hierarchical power that would create a better church.

One could also imagine that while this particular finance committee performed courageously under pressure, finance committees in general would be more able to serve the church if they included representatives who were elected by the laity, as would all structures for lay participation called for by Vatican II.

While I was struggling with the problem of church governance, I mentioned at one of our meetings that we should consider writing a constitution for the exercise of power by the laity in the church. While the word *constitution* shocked a few of our members, someone reported that a group had actually been working for decades on such a task. I thus learned of the work led by Leonard Swidler, professor of religion at Temple University in Philadelphia. I spoke with Professor Swidler, who was most helpful and interested in our group.

Swidler and his colleagues in the Association for the Rights of Catholics in the Church had given much thought to topics that were novel to us. They had articulated the reasons for greater distribution of power within the church, and suggested structures that would inject democratic practices at many levels. I saw much in their advocacy of democracy that I shared, but I also realized that Voice was taking a very different approach. The group's Web site (www.arcc-catholic-rights.org) contained a list of thirty-two rights that many would advocate but many others would oppose. It seemed to me that this broader agenda would limit support for the creation of a democratic process. In addition, their constitution applied to the whole church, not just the laity. Finally, their path called for the laity to petition the hierarchy to create such processes—an approach I thought the hierarchy would block because groups rarely support actions that will diminish their own power.

Our evolving strategy was to remain narrowly focused and to initiate our own democratic processes. For this we did not need approval from the hierarchy, since we were simply creating a mechanism by which the laity could accept the responsibilities they were called to assume by the teachings of Vatican II.

—IV—

As word spread that Voice of the Faithful was seeking a Catholic "democracy," we were repeatedly told that the Catholic Church is *not* a democracy. To this we replied that we were creating a democracy for only one component of the church—the laity. And we did not intend to vote on dogma; we accepted the core teachings of the faith. Nor did we want to dominate the hierarchy; we sought partnership.

I had some troubles as a newcomer to this discussion on church structure. In early discussions about Voice with Father Tom, he had said we needed to consult with experts on "ecclesiology"—a word I had never heard but understood its meaning as the study of ecclesial, or church, structure.

And then I described the wrong structure to 10 million people. Two months after we started, CNN asked if I would describe our organization in a live interview with Aaron Brown. Thinking this would be an excellent way to spread the good news of this new democracy for the laity to Catholics, I accepted.

A black limousine was sent to the St. John's school parking lot to rush me directly from the weekly Voice happening to a Studio in Boston in time for the 11 P.M. news. I sat alone in the back of the limo as we sped to the studio. The heavily cushioned black leather seat gave me the feeling that I was a diplomat on an important mission. I was exhausted from the pace of the prior two months, and from just having led a contentious three-hour meeting. The cumulative stress of four or five meetings per week and hundreds of daily e-mails was taking its toll.

The night watchman let us into the studio. I was led to a small dark room and seated with a map of the Boston skyline behind me. The technician attached a microphone to my tie and gave me an earpiece to wear, through which someone told me to look straight ahead at a black wall and "stand by." It was all very peaceful, and I began to fall asleep.

I was then brought back to full consciousness by the voice of Aaron Brown, the CNN anchor. He described the scandal in Boston, and introduced me as the president of a newly formed group of laity. I told him it had been quite an evening. He then asked about our analysis of the problem and noted that the Catholic Church is not a democracy.

I replied that the Catholic Church is composed of both hierarchy and laity, and we were working with the laity, who needed a voice. Still foggy, I then added, for millions to hear, that "the problem with the Catholic Church is that the laity has too much power." After a pause in which he pondered this colossal misstatement, he politely asked, "Doctor, do you mean the *hierarchy* has too much power?"

"Yes, yes, that is what I meant to say."

Remembering my error, for weeks I cringed every time I watched CNN.

—⚏—

The Catholic Church did not start out with an imperial style. On the contrary, as noted by Father Tom Doyle, Christ lived his ministry according to a democratic ideal and specifically recommended a democratic structure for human organizations. Although there are disputes among scholars on the exact historical words of Jesus, remarkably similar citations in support of democracy are available from two of the Evangelists, Matthew and Mark. The Lord said to the quarrelling apostles,

> *You know that the rulers of the Gentiles lord it over them, and their great men exercise authority over them. It shall not be so among you; but whoever would be great among you must be your servant and whoever would be first among you must be your slave even as the Son of man came not to be served but to serve.* (Matthew 20:25–28)

And from Mark,

> *You know that in the world the recognized rulers lord it over their subjects, and their great men make them feel the weight of authority. This is not the way with you; among you, whoever wants to be great must be your servant, and whoever wants to be the first must be the willing slave of all.* (Mark 10: 42–43)

But there are also direct statements attributed to Christ in support of a powerful central authority. The statement of Christ that "Thou art Peter and upon this rock I shall build my Church . . ." (Matt. 16:18) is often cited in support of a powerful papacy. In light of the massive failure of current church governance, Catholics must now resolve these apparently conflicting views on centralized versus grassroots power.

I believe that both democracy and centralized power are essential features of the hybrid church structure advocated by Vatican II and Voice of the Faithful. The hierarchy rightly traces its heritage and mandate to the statements of Christ to St. Peter. The source of authority of the laity is their participation in priestly duties through their baptism, and the concept of a pilgrim church (as articulated in the documents of Vatican II) that must learn and improve though history. Democracy is the vehicle through which the experience of the laity with the world can be refined and brought, in communion with the hierarchy, to the entire church.

— V —

There is abundant evidence that the early church struck an excellent balance between centralized leadership and the voice of the faithful. Even before the institutional church began to form, Jesus Christ could have acted as an autocratic ruler. Instead, he preached and lived a message of humility, love, and inclusiveness far different from that modeled by some current members of the hierarchy. And, among his earliest followers, the predecessors of the current church hierarchy, there was a general recognition that "whoever wants to be the first must be the willing slave of all." St. Paul in his letter to the Corinthians indicated his respect for all the faithful with the statement that "to each is given the manifestation of the spirit for the common good" (I Corinthians 12).

As the members of Voice studied the early church, we were encouraged to find that there was much less differentiation between clergy, hierarchy, and laity than currently exists. By the third century, when bishops became increasingly important figures, the laity continued to have an important role and actually participated in their selection. Today, bishops are named by a distant pope with no formal consultation with the laity.

While the Bishop of Rome, as the successor of Peter, held special importance and extra influence because of his location in the administrative center of the Roman Empire, bishops and theologians from many locations made major contributions to the intellectual life of the church. The papacy in that early period, represented by the Bishop of Rome, did not control all the Catholic followers of Jesus, nor did it cloak itself in the style and garments of an emperor. It was a peoples' church, united in each location around its bishop with diverse groups of Catholics struggling, in a largely decentralized manner, to understand the revolutionary teachings of Christ. Within these small groups there was no isolated, all-powerful hierarchy that could permit individual bishops, in secret actions, to protect pedophilic priests and move them from one group of the faithful to another.

The assumption of excessive power by the leaders of the Catholic Church began with a stunning historical event: the conversion of the Roman emperor Constantine to Catholicism in 312. James Carroll, the former priest and author, wrote a riveting book about this dramatic transformation of Catholicism, called *Constantine's Sword*. The story is that Constantine sought to conquer Rome, which was controlled by his rival Maxentius, who worshiped a different pagan deity. Carroll reports that while Constantine sought the encounter, his legions were demoralized and concerned about going into battle so far from home. They would be the decided underdog. But the night before the battle, Constantine saw a cross in the sky above the legend *In Hoc Signo Vinces* ("In This Sign, Conquer"). With the news of this vision—a signal of favor from the Christian God—Constantine's troops rallied, went into battle the next day, and won. Constantine himself threw Maxentius off the Milvian Bridge into the Tiber River, where he drowned. Carroll notes that "on the strength of that vision and its fulfillment, the emperor became a Christian; so did his army and, ultimately, so did the empire."

Carroll then gives his view of the importance of the event in the development of Western civilization. "After the death and

Resurrection of Jesus, the conversion of Constantine may have been the most implication-laden event in Western history. If we rarely think so, that is because we take utterly for granted the structures of culture, mind, politics, spirituality, and even calendar (Sunday as holiday) to which it led. When the power of the empire became joined to the ideology of the church, both institutions were changed—for better and for worse."

Constantine then sought to extend his military rule, and to establish spiritual domination as well. In 313 he wrote to his prefect in Africa that in regard to the Donatists, a group of Christians identified as schismatics, he would like to "see all venerating the most holy God in the proper cult of the catholic religion." And in 325 he summoned more than three hundred bishops to a meeting in Nicaea to resolve their differences. This meeting, over which he presided, led to the Nicene Creed with its familiar lines that we still recite today: "We believe in one God, the Father, the almighty, maker of heaven and earth, . . . We believe in one holy, catholic, and apostolic Church . . ."

The call for religious uniformity issued by an all-powerful emperor and overseen by a recognized hierarchy can be viewed as a benefit in preserving the core truths of Catholicism. But it also established a concentration of power that presented what Carroll describes as the perennial human problem: "how to keep the ideal of unity free of the burden of tyranny."

So the conversion and subsequent actions of Constantine had many long-lasting effects on the church. It became easy to be a Christian, since the religion was legitimized, and numbers increased greatly. The role of bishops was increased, which created the precondition for the emergence of the papacy. And finally a process was set in motion that over the centuries would lead to enhanced power of the hierarchy. In view of the present-day struggle of the laity for even a minimal voice in church governance, it is ironic that Constantine accomplished all of this as a non-Catholic who became a member of the laity with his deathbed conversion.

—៣—

The first major change in the centralized structure established by Constantine was a massive split into two parts. This division occurred as a consequence of the collapse of the Roman Empire in 476. After Rome fell, the eastern portion of the empire continued on as the Byzantine Empire. In this new secular situation, the Catholic patriarch in Constantinople served at the pleasure of the ruler of the Byzantine Empire and did not report directly to Rome. This led to great tension between these two branches of Christendom that culminated in a schismatic break between Roman Catholicism and Orthodoxy in 1054. While the Roman Catholic Church continued on with its strong papacy and emphasis on centralized power, the Orthodox tradition adopted a less centralized manner with development of the familiar Greek and Russian Orthodox churches.

In the Roman Catholic Church, governance evolved with an ebb and flow of power between the bishop of Rome, who emerged as pope, and councils of the church composed of bishops, archbishops, and cardinals. The power of the papacy was codified by the proclamation *Dictates of the Pope*, thought to be written by Pope Gregory VII in 1075. This document asserts that papal authority is above secular authority. Dictate 19 states, "He [the pope] may be judged by no one." As expected, the proclamation led to disagreement between the pope and Emperor Henry IV that resulted in an external conflict for the church. Within the church, the Gregorian reform asserted the supremacy of the pope, with power limited to some degree by the electoral system and the need to accommodate influential bishops who remained powerful within their dioceses, with strong support from the local aristocracy. The minimal level of checks and balances was quite similar to that existing in the modern church. In 1302, Boniface VIII claimed even greater power for the papacy in the document *Unam Sanctam*, which stated that to be saved, an individual must be subject to the Roman pontiff.

The effectiveness of the path toward clearly defined dogma and centralized rule initiated by Constantine, and further developed in the Roman church by Gregory VII and Boniface VIII, is undeniable—the Catholic Church has brought the message of Christ to billions of individuals for almost two thousand years. Indeed, autocratic structures can accomplish certain missions, but they are also prone to abuses of power, and they do not provide the church with a mechanism to accomplish orderly change in response to developments in the secular world that are best known by the laity.

—VI—

The recent sex abuse scandal provides a striking view of the dark underside of the autocratic practices of Catholicism. But the thousand-year interaction of the centralized Catholic Church with the external world provides other moments of revelation in which both its good and evil effects are revealed.

In the thirteenth century the great Catholic theologian Saint Thomas Aquinas, while studying in Paris, began to incorporate the ideas of Aristotle into the Catholic tradition. Aristotle sought to promote science "as sure and evident knowledge obtained from demonstrations." Aquinas then spoke of "knowledge of things from their causes." Both acknowledged that humanity would be engaged in a continual pursuit of new knowledge of the world. For Saint Thomas, living in the Catholic tradition, an Aristotelian search for knowledge would support changes in the church, or doctrinal development, as new information was obtained.

In fact, during the Middle Ages there was strong papal support for education. The *Catholic Encyclopedia* reports that from 1400 to 1506 the popes granted charters to nearly thirty universities, including such famous institutions as the University of Paris. The intellectual ferment in these religious-based universities led to important developments in science and the humanities, including the flowering of arts in the Renaissance in northern Italy.

The education of a larger number of individuals would eventually lead to a demand for the separation of church and state, for modern political democracies, and for a larger role for the laity in the affairs of the church. A critical ingredient for the development of this mass consciousness was the invention of the printing press by Johannes Gutenberg, whose first product was a Bible, printed in 1455. The invention of printing encouraged the growth of democratic thinking and facilitated the spread of ideas that would alter the development of the church.

While the work of Thomas Aquinas and papal support for education were positive developments, deficiencies of the Church were also evident. For example, in my review of the medieval period of the church I was startled to learn the full story of Joan of Arc, the saint for whom my grade school in Indianapolis, Indiana, was named. Like most Catholics, and certainly those from St. Joan of Arc Grade School, I knew the basic story. Joan of Arc at age seventeen received a vision in which she was told that she should lead the French army against the English force occupying France at the time. She was successful in battle but was later burned at the stake and subsequently canonized.

I came to learn that her death was related to the entanglement of church and state at that time. She was captured by the English and in 1430 was tried at a tribunal presided over by the infamous Bishop Cauchon, who hoped that the English would help him become archbishop.

The bishop needed damning evidence for the trial, and he stooped to a final baseness to obtain it: a priest who pretended to come from the region of Joan's own home and to be a friend was smuggled into her cell, and he misused his sacred office to steal her confidence; she confided to him the things that her prosecutors had tried in vain to trick her into betraying. A concealed accomplice wrote it all down and delivered it to Cauchon.

Because of this information, Joan of Arc was burned at the stake at the age of nineteen. The great American writer Mark Twain describes her last moments (see www.catholic-forum.com/saints):

When the fires rose about her and she begged for a cross for her dying lips to kiss, it was not a friend but an enemy, not a Frenchman but an alien, not a comrade in arms but an English soldier, that answered her pathetic prayer. He broke a stick across his knee, bound the pieces together in the form of the symbol she so loved, and gave it her; and his gentle deed is not forgotten, nor will be.

Twenty-five years later, the Catholic hierarchy instituted a Process of Rehabilitation of Joan of Arc, and in 1920—in an extreme example of a policy reversal—the Catholic Church canonized the young girl its hierarchy had helped burn to death as a heretic.

The Crusades in the twelfth century, the Inquisition in the sixteenth, and the sexual abuses of children in the twentieth century are further examples of errors committed by a religious structure that bestows absolute, unchecked power upon fallible humans. The question Voice of the Faithful poses is, Will it be possible, with the active participation of the laity, to create a better church that will not be destined to commit another round of atrocities?

— VII —

The fifteenth and sixteenth centuries, with rising levels of education and the invention of printing on the one hand, and massive corruption of the church exemplified by the burning and subsequent rehabilitation of Joan of Arc on the other, were a time of major change in the Catholic Church. In this critical and fluid moment, with massive historic forces poised to alter the fifteen-hundred-year-old institution founded by Jesus Christ, a courageous Augustinian monk, Martin Luther, stepped forth to offer his ideas.

At Saint Joan of Arc Grade School I had been taught that Lutherans were fallen Catholics and should be avoided. But my early role in Voice led me to be compared to Martin Luther. The spring 2003 issue of the Notre Dame alumni magazine carried a letter to the editor attacking me as an egotist whose reliance on doing things my way reminded the writer of Luther. People asked me if I were advocating a split with the church similar to that caused by Luther. A friend even jokingly wondered if there would someday be Mullerans. I quickly replied that I was just one of many cofounders of Voice of the Faithful and that none of us had any interest in creating a separate church. We all wanted to improve the Catholic Church, not leave it.

Martin Luther posted his famous ninety-five propositions for debate on the door of the Castle Chapel in Wittenberg, Germany, in 1517. It was a time in which indulgences, or reductions in the penance due for sins, were being sold by the hierarchy. In Luther's diocese, half of the proceeds would be sent to Rome to finance the very expensive construction of St. Peter's Cathedral, whose opulence he had noted on a recent visit. Luther questioned whether the relatively poor German Church should be exporting money to Italy.

However, Luther's objections were more theological than economic. He objected in principle to the idea that salvation could be obtained through the intercession of the church or even by the actions of an individual. He believed that salvation was the gift of a loving God and that the purchase of indulgences from the church contradicted that item of faith. Of course, the sale of indulgences was supported by the local bishop and the pope, and Luther found himself in conflict with the authority of the church. While Luther did not seek to leave the church, his fundamental objections to its operation, his location in Germany, which had nationalistic forces supporting a split from Italian influence, a widespread disaffection with the current state of the church, and the rigidity of the church's response to its corruption in the Middle Ages, led to the tragic split. The readiness for change was further indicated by the rapid emergence of other movements that led to the Calvinist, Presbyterian, Congregational, Anglican, and other branches of Christianity.

In the sixteenth century, Luther did not have the means to communicate effectively with a large enough number of the laity and other theologians to create the critical mass necessary to change the church from the grassroots level. With little prospect for change, a split became unavoidable. Today, with the tools of mass education, the Internet, e-mail, a free and effective press, and democratic processes, Catholics have a much better chance of changing the way the church acts than Luther.

Scott Appleby, the church historian from Notre Dame, was quoted in the *New York Times* in the spring of 2002 as saying that Voice is more like Erasmus than Luther. While I conduct heart research with scientific colleagues at Erasmus University in Rotterdam, I knew nothing of the theological contributions of Erasmus to the Catholic Church. I therefore purchased *In Praise of Folly*, his satirical work about the same corruption of the church in the sixteenth century that had prompted his contemporary, Luther, to take action.

Despite his use of strong language, Erasmus did not favor a break with the papacy, nor did he directly challenge church doctrine as did Luther. He sought to describe the problems of the church so that it might return to the message of Christ. He advocated more careful study of the original Gospel texts, which he studied in the original as a biblical scholar, and a return to the practices of the early church. When a critic said that his criticism was too harsh to be useful, and that he "wounded the delicate ear with sharp-edged truth," he defended the telling of unpleasant truths as a means to improve the church.

In our current crisis, the public statements by survivors and the skilled reporting by the *Boston Globe* and other media, are contributions in accord with the truth-telling legacy of

Erasmus. I believe that Scott Appleby is right in comparing Voice of the Faithful to Erasmus's approach, and predict that as it matures—and historical perspective becomes available— Voice will continue to deserve this great honor. But it will not be truth-telling by an individual—it will be the presentation of truth as discerned by the laity as a whole, distilled and refined by the laity's use of democratic practices.

—VIII—

Despite the moderate approach of Erasmus and the desire of Luther to remain within the church, their activities were followed by schism. The papacy, which was under attack as the Reformation gathered strength, reacted in a defensive manner. The central office of the Inquisition was strengthened, and a papal council was convened in Trent from 1544 to 1563. While the Council made many internal improvements regarding indulgences, religious education, discipline, and the sacraments, there was little consideration of the reform of the papacy. In contrast to the true ecumenical council of Vatican II, the Council of Trent was primarily a council to create reforms required for the struggle against the Reformation.

This left Western civilization with a new basis for religious wars, which further discredited religion and contributed to the separation of secular from religious life. It also meant that a unique opportunity for church reform was lost, with many of the potential agents of change leaving the church.

While the post-Reformation church reemphasized its top-down, autocratic structure, there arose a steadily advancing knowledge of the world that resulted from the development of the scientific method. The growing conflict between the church and science peaked with the assertions of Galileo in the early seventeenth century. As a medical scientist trained to seek increased knowledge of the world, I was particularly interested in the relationship of Catholic teaching to the scientific findings of Galileo. In 1998 I had somewhat mischievously chosen this topic for a commencement address at Bellarmine College in Kentucky because the school's namesake, Cardinal Robert Bellarmine, had been involved in the investigation of Galileo. The college administration was relieved that I noted the role Cardinal Bellarmine played in diminishing the persecution of Galileo.

Galileo was born in 1564, well after the start of the Reformation, and rose to become a highly respected mathematician and friend of cardinals and popes. With newly improved lenses he created a telescope that magnified celestial objects fourteenfold, allowing him to scan the heavens and see more of God's creation than had any other human. He discovered moons around Jupiter, different phases of the planet Venus, and craters on our moon indicating that celestial collisions had occurred. He realized that this evidence of motion in the solar system supported the proposal of Copernicus that the earth, which the church taught was fixed in the center of the universe, actually moved around the sun.

In 1632, at the age of sixty-eight, in an era in which heresy might lead to death at the stake, he was tried by the church for his continued assertion that Copernicus was correct. After reviewing his case, a committee of cardinals issued the following official opinion.

> We say, pronounce, sentence, and declare that you, Galileo, by reason of these things which have been detailed in the trial and which you have confessed already, have rendered yourself according to this Holy Office vehemently suspect of heresy, namely of having held and believed a doctrine that is false and contrary to the divine and Holy Scripture: namely that Sun is the centre of the world and does not move from east to west, and that one may hold and defend as probable an opinion after it has been declared and defined contrary to Holy Scripture. . . . We condemn you to formal imprisonment in this Holy Office at our pleasure.

For providing critical information on the nature of the material world, Galileo was rewarded with condemnation and house arrest for his remaining years.

Over the ensuing centuries, church leaders developed a respect for the information about the material world that culminated in the foundation of the Pontifical Academy of Sciences in 1936 by Pius XI. The academy was to serve as a "resource upon which the Holy See and its various bodies can draw." Today it is composed of many distinguished lay scientists, such as Dr. Joseph Murray, the winner of the Nobel Prize in Medicine for his work on organ transplantation, who is also a leader of Voice of the Faithful. In 1992 the Pontifical Academy issued a report on the Galileo affair, which led the church to issue an official apology to Galileo 360 years after his condemnation.

This closure on the Galileo issue is an accurate sign that the Catholic Church, with its great respect for education and belief in doctrinal development, now is well equipped to assimilate new information about the physical universe as it becomes available. Pontifical academy astronomers are among world leaders in the study of cosmology.

While the paths through which new knowledge of the physical world can be incorporated into evolving church teachings are now well developed, the path by which progress in the less precise spheres of sociology, political science, philosophy, and other social sciences can reach the church is severely consticted and progress is slow. This is the defect in discernment that an organized, democratic structure for the laity can correct. Voice can, by identifying the collective wisdom of the laity in all aspects of their lives, provide the church with refined input of new social, ethical, and spiritual views, in a way that parallels reporting by the Pontifical Academy of Science on the physical world.

— IX —

The respect for the individual that began with the Renaissance in the fifteenth century accelerated in the eighteenth century with the growth of science and the Enlightenment. Rather than looking to the church for an understanding of the great questions of human existence, thinkers such as Voltaire argued that the universe progressed without continued divine intervention. A measure of immortality could be gained not through resurrection facilitated by the church, but by contributing to the forward progress of the human race. Man, not God, was advocated as the measure of all things. Reason was accorded greater importance than faith. Individuals had rights that even kings and popes should not violate, and such rights should be the basis of government. The flaws of man, which Enlightenment thinkers acknowledged, could be accommodated by designing human institutions in such a manner that corruptible individuals could not have access to excessive power.

These revolutionary ideas, which originated in Europe, would be embodied in the founding of the democratic government of the United States of America. The American Revolution was a movement against a monarchial style of government. Founding Fathers such as Adams, Madison, Franklin, and Jefferson were well aware of the writings of Montesquieu, Hobbes, and other Enlightenment leaders. They wanted to create a government of checks and balances in which the dangerous power of the state could be exercised with safety. They had also seen the abuses of power associated with the union of church and state, and they insisted on their separation.

The idea that Americans must assert their independence from England flourished in Virginia, Pennsylvania, New York, and other colonies. But it was the people of Boston, in 1775, who saw the need for a new form of government so clearly that the first shots of the Revolutionary War were fired. Likewise, in the twenty-first century the citizens of Boston would take a special pride in offering democracy as a component of government, not in the secular world but for the laity of the Catholic Church.

It is clear that the church of the eighteenth and nineteenth centuries had much to fear from democracy. In the wake of the French Revolution, which espoused many of the ideals of the American Revolution, many members of the hierarchy were killed, churches were ruined, and sacred texts were defiled. Church leaders in Rome, then, became sensitized to any suggestion of democratic practices in the American Catholic Church, and they subsequently spoke out on the evil of "Americanism." As had occurred during the Reformation, secular challenges to the church led paradoxically to a strengthening in its autocratic nature.

I had always assumed that papal infallibility had been a constant throughout church history. But I was surprised to learn that the doctrine was greatly enhanced in 1870, and under unusual circumstances. In his book *Papal Sin*, Garry Wills describes the manner in which Pius IX sought to strengthen the principle of papal infallibility at the First Vatican Council, 1869–70. Years prior to the council, Pius IX had issued a statement proclaiming the Immaculate Conception of Mary—the doctrine that she was conceived without original sin. This was a popular teaching, and one that if issued as infallible would have the indirect result of supporting the concept of papal infallibility.

As Garry describes it, Pius IX had been driven from Rome by secular forces and sealed in Vatican City. From this position of siege, he sought to firm up his papal authority, which like that of kings and princes was under assault by forces labeled as "modern." Since the hierarchy knew that Pius IX wanted a decision in favor of infallibility but also that dissent from some quarters was likely, the rule was established that a simple majority vote of those attending the council would be sufficient for approval.

Wills notes that there was considerable opposition in the preliminary vote, and most of those in opposition then left for home. When the final vote was taken, only two negative votes were cast, and papal infallibility became an official position of the Roman Catholic Church. But dissent with the vote remained. In referring to the papacy and its enhanced powers, Lord Acton would make his famous statement, "Power corrupts, and absolute power corrupts absolutely."

While infallibility has been invoked for only two teachings—in support of Mary's Immaculate Conception, and her Assumption into Heaven—the mere existence of the principle has created a halo of infallibility over many fallible assertions by the pope and others, and an "infallibility creep" has occurred. Father Donald Cozzens has noted the distinction between "official truth," which represents infallible statements of the church, and "common truth," which is dependent on the historical conditions of the church and subject to change. A decision by a bishop to close an inner-city school is not part of the official truth of the church—it represents part of the common truth in which the laity have an important perspective to offer. Yet such a decision is frequently issued in an autocratic manner.

The term *cafeteria Catholic* has been used to disparage a believer who accepts only those church teachings with which he or she agrees. And yet in the Middle Ages, the church tolerated slavery, taught that the earth was the immovable center of the universe, and burned to death those who disagreed with it. A lay person who disagreed with those fallible teachings of the church could have helped the church acquire the truth more rapidly.

Extended infallibility also hampers problem solving. To be solved, a problem must first be acknowledged. But within an institution burdened by maintaining its aura of infallibility, serious problems have been suppressed to avoid scandal. Unfortunately, we have learned too well that a scandal suppressed only prolongs pain and suffering.

—X—

The Second Vatican Council convened in 1962, a wonderful moment for American Catholics. John F. Kennedy had just been elected by people of many faiths to be the first Catholic president of the United States. And the council created a sense that the church was awakening from its medieval slumber and finally responding to the call for more of a voice for the laity.

I was surprised to learn from the speech of James Carroll at our convention that the Holocaust was a major factor in the momentous decision of Pope John XXIII to convene Vatican II. Catholic guards had executed children in the concentration camps. Some clergy had actively associated with Nazis. The pope during World War II, Pius XII, had been the Vatican ambassador to Germany in the 1930s. He therefore had considerable knowledge about the Nazi regime. Why did he fail to bring the maximum force of the papacy to the aid of the Jews? And did the teachings of the church about the crucifixion of Christ contribute to anti-Semitism?

The church did not respond immediately to the teachings of the council. Father Donald Cozzens, in *The Sacred Silence*, reports that even as Vatican II was in progress, as a seminarian he was required to take an oath against modernism. He had to pledge to resist the evolution of church dogma based on the experience of humans and the church in the world, which was interpreted by some as a mandate to resist all change. But it was clearly Pope John XXIII's hope that Vatican II's opening the doors of the church to the modern world would result in an improved church.

Anthony Massimini, a former priest and a leader of Voice of the Faithful who attended Vatican II, has spoken eloquently of his sense that the dialogue that occurred there had been inspired by the Holy Spirit. Democratic processes governed the drafting and approval of documents. Many critics of prior church practices, who had been attacked in the assault against modernism, were invited to participate in the preparation of documents for the Council. The Decree on Ecumenism II stated, "Christ summons (the Church) to continual reformation as she sojourns here on earth. The church is always in need of this, insofar as she is an institution of men here on earth."

I graduated from Notre Dame in 1965, excited by the many ideas expressed at Vatican II, which ended that year. The council was explicit that the church must be open to change: to return to the teachings of Christ, to dialogue with other faiths, to encourage social activism that supports education, health care, and work for the poor. The most immediate and visible legacies of Vatican II were the change in the mass from Latin into the vernacular, and the turning of the altar so that the priest faced the people. Both of these highlighted the importance of the active participation of the people of God in the service—a "democratization" of the liturgy.

But such sweeping changes were not without their critics, and the years following Vatican II were rife with debate between traditionalists and progressives. My uncle Father Paul Courtney, who was in his fifties at the time of Vatican II, was one of the dissenters. He was a pious man who valued the mystical communication with divinity that was facilitated by the Latin mass. He did not want the church converted into a community group that pursued worthy causes. When the time in the mass came for the people to turn to each other and exchange a handshake of peace, he would say, "You may now visit with your neighbor—if you must."

Today, both traditional and progressive Catholics urge greater adherence to the principles of Vatican II, although different teachings are emphasized. Traditionalists stress the recognition of papal primacy expressed by the council, while progressives seek an increased role of the rank-and-file faithful in church affairs. The debate has even spilled over to the recent scandal. Traditionalists have blamed a lack of discipline for the crimes, while progressives believe that secrecy and resistance by the hierarchy to lay influence contributed to the problem.

While the decades after the Second Vatican Council have been a time of valuable debate on the nature of the church, marked differences remain and constructive dialogue has been limited. It is my hope that all laity—traditionalists, progressives, and the biggest group of Catholics, moderates—will find Voice of the Faithful a viable forum in which to debate the issues raised most recently as well as those that predated the sexual abuse scandal.

— XI —

Forty years after Vatican II, the idea that a stronger, more democratic voice for the laity was needed had emerged in Boston, the birthplace of the American Revolution. Whenever I noted this, the audience at Voice meetings in Boston came to life and applauded. We knew that sexual abuse scandals had occurred in other dioceses in the 1980s and 1990s. But in these cases the problem of sexual abuse had been addressed narrowly, without efforts to identify or correct the underlying problem. Boston, we determined, would be different—we would address the abuse of power and offer democracy as a remedy.

As our organization grew and our goals became apparent, I began to note amazing parallels between the birth of American democracy and the beginnings of a democracy for the Catholic laity. The Boston Tea Party was analogous to the work of the press, the trial lawyers, and the survivors who had taken a courageous public stand against a concealed abuse. A parish in Lexington, where the first shot of the Revolutionary War had been fired, had, prior to Voice, withheld funds until an incompetent pastor had been removed. And Concord, where the second battle of the Revolution occurred, was the town with the first group to establish a Voice affiliate after our founding at St. John's. I felt that our task, in establishing our own council and governance structure, was similar to that of the Constitutional Convention.

It was a joy to discuss these analogies with the Boston-area Catholics who came weekly to our meetings. You could sense their joy that out of the tragic scandal that had revealed the flaws of their church, they might add democracy—a jewel in which New Englanders took great pride—to the structure of the church. This sense of purpose energized our meetings and sustained us through countless hours of preparation for our convention—a joyous, democratic moment at which the will of the laity was so beautifully expressed.

CHAPTER 10

THE BATTLE IS JOINED

— I —

THE CONVENTION transformed our movement.

With this one event we demonstrated the determination of an active laity to play a serious role in the affairs of the church. While this was uplifting to countless lay Catholics, it was viewed through a darker, more ominous lens by some within the hierarchy. Some church leaders viewed an empowered Voice of the Faithful as a threat to their power, and it quickly became clear that they would now try to destroy our organization.

The glow of the Saturday convention lasted less than forty-eight hours. Late Monday afternoon, July 22, 2002, Cardinal Law and his followers launched a public assault on Voice that would last for months. The astonishing thing about it to me—both then and now—was that church leaders were mounting a planned, deliberate attack on mainstream, active Catholics. A cardinal and his aides were plotting against men and women whose Catholic faith was a central part of their lives. Jim Post would later say that this action by the Cardinal amounted to a "declaration of war" on Voice of the Faithful.

To me, it was a third scandal. The first scandal, of course, had been the sexual abuse of children by priests; the second had been the cover-up of that abuse by many in the hierarchy. And this third scandal, clearly in the making, was the effort by some in the hierarchy to undermine and destroy an organization of lay Catholics whose only goal was to rebuild and improve the church after the sex abuse tragedy.

Our success had been too great. Our convention had come off too well. We were too strong. We had demonstrated that our movement had breadth and depth and potentially real staying power. We were now more than a theoretical threat to the power of the hierarchy.

And so on that Monday afternoon, Cardinal Law announced that he would not accept our donations, intended for a variety of causes ranging from schools to hospitals. The reason given was that our efforts to raise funds would undermine the cardinal's efforts to do so. We had, in fact, been quite careful to say to people, If you want to donate to the cardinal, please do so, but if you are reluctant to do so—and many people were for obvious reasons—then we will accept your donation and see that it reaches those in need. We pledged to donors that their money would not be used for secret settlements or PR campaigns by the archdiocese.

The cardinal's spokesman told the press that our fund-raising work did not "recognize the role of the archbishop and his responsibility in providing for the various programs and activities of the church."

It was an echo of the meeting we had had back in the spring with Bishop Edyvean when Father O'Connell had angrily denounced our fund-raising efforts on the grounds that only the bishop had the power to raise such funds. To members of Voice, it was clear that at the heart of the cardinal's action was the desire to maximize his power. How else is it possible to explain why he would turn down funds intended for those who need help most? How does a man of God intentionally reduce rather than increase the amount of money available for the poor?

The notion that we were somehow interfering with the relationship between the Cardinal and the faithful was absurd. We were a part of the faithful. The real reason that the Cardinal's Appeal was failing miserably was that he had mishandled the sexual abuse scandal.

Others came to our defense, including survivors' groups. David Clohessy, national director of the Survivors Network of those Abused by Priests, told the press, "I never thought I would see the day when any Catholic official advocated any roadblock in helping the poor. The mission of the church is to help the needy in every way possible."

The archdiocesan spokesman, Father Christopher Coyne, said that rejecting our donations was "in no way" an indication that the church was trying to harm our organization. Father Coyne said that archdiocesan officials were engaged in "good and fruitful talks" with Voice. But the truth was that we were *not* engaged in talks with the archdiocese at that time.

Paul Baier and Svea—both on a high from the convention—were shocked by the attack from the Cardinal. Svea, in particular was reeling, for the assault came literally less than twenty-four hours after she had placed a call to the chancery and left a message on Cardinal Law's voice mail commending him for his response to to Arthur Austin.

"It was one step forward and ten steps back," said Svea. "Just when you think there's a glimmer of hope, a softening, an opening—it gets slammed shut. That was stunning."

At our regular Monday meeting that night there was a sense of utter disbelief. People came expecting to join in the afterglow, anticipating lively chatter about how wonderful the convention had been, and instead were informed of the latest news.

When the hierarchy turned down the donation, the money was offered to Catholic Charities, one of the largest social services agencies in Massachusetts. Catholic Charities is under the administrative control of the hierarchy, and it is a traditional organization that is generally deferential to the Cardinal. Yet there were a number of prominent people on the board who had the courage to stand up to the Cardinal—including Chairman Neal Finnegan and Vice Chairman Peter Meade. These were prominent people in the business community who understood politics, who knew the city well and had given much of their time to making it a better place. Thus, Catholic Charities announced that it would accept our donation. A number of Catholic Charities board members publicly expressed their displeasure with the Cardinal's decision not to accept our contributions. Thomas P. O'Neill III, former Massachusetts lieutenant governor, said he thought it appropriate that Catholic Charities accept our donations. He told reporters that "Some people, in light of the scandal, are just choosing to financially boycott the Cardinal's Appeal, and Voice of the Faithful is trying to fill the void to make sure social services for the poor are maintained."

David Castaldi, one of our members and a man who had served with distinction in a major finance role for the archdiocese, said: "We don't want to compete with the Cardinal's Appeal; we want to supplement it."

By the end of the week, the Archdiocesan newspaper *The Pilot*, which was under the firm control of Cardinal Law, published a scathing attack on our convention. We were criticized because one of the speakers (out of more than fifty speakers in all) at our convention was involved with a Catholic group in

Germany called We Are Church, which advocated liberal positions such as permitting priests to marry. Ergo, the article indicated, our movement should be viewed with suspicion.

— I I —

As we faced what was to be a period of sustained adversity, we were fortified by talented people with experience in contentious public battles. Jim Post, as our president, was on the front lines for this difficult period. We were blessed that Jim had the skills and commitment to protect Voice during this intense attack by the hierarchy.

Like so many others within our group, Jim was a lifelong Catholic. He had grown up in Buffalo, New York, the son of a State Farm Insurance salesman. Jim was an altar boy, a devoted Catholic. After high school he received a scholarship to St. Bonaventure College, a Franciscan school sixty miles south of Buffalo. He graduated in 1965 and received a scholarship to Villanova Law School in Philadelphia, where he met his future wife, Jeannette, also a Catholic, who was then in medical school. After law school, Jim returned to upstate New York where he completed the MBA program. In the process, he found that he enjoyed teaching and decided to enter a doctoral program. He joined the faculty of Boston University in 1975 and earned his Ph.D. a year later from the State University of New York.

Jim had a distinguished academic record as a professor of management and public policy at Boston University. He is the author or coauthor of fifteen books, including the leading textbook in its field, *Business and Society: Corporate Strategy, Public Policy, and Ethics* (with Professors Anne T. Lawrence and James Weber), which is now in its tenth edition. Throughout his career, Jim has focused on how institutions adapt to change—a specialty that made him ideally suited to play a prominent role in Voice of the Faithful.

In the late 1970s, Jim joined a then fledgling effort to deal with the problem of American companies selling—or giving away free, as a marketing tactic—powdered baby formula in developing nations. The powdered formula required both clean water and literacy—two things often missing in those countries. If either is absent, there can be great danger to the baby receiving the formula. Working with the Rockefeller Foundation and the World Health Organization, Jim sought to expose what American companies were doing and get them to stop. It was clear that breast-feeding in the vast majority of instances was far healthier and less expensive than using the formula. But the companies—led by Nestlé—persisted.

The Nestlé Infant Formula Audit Commission was formed, headed by Senator Edmund Muskie of Maine. Jim Post was named to the commission and traveled the world seeing firsthand the effects of the formula problem. In a hospital ward in Indonesia he saw fifty infants who had gotten sick because of improper use of formula. All were under a year old, and some did not survive. He saw similarly sorrowful scenes in other nations, including Colombia and Thailand. Jim played a key role in the consumer boycott of the Nestlé Company, which lasted for seven years and ultimately led to a variety of reforms, including Nestlé accepting the World Health Organization code of conduct for marketing infant formula.

—⚏—

As the battle lines between Cardinal Law and Voice of the Faithful were drawn, we were not only blessed with the experienced leadership of Jim Post, we were also buoyed by support from survivors' groups, from many priests and nuns, from the press, and from theologians and intellectuals. It was particularly heartening to read the words of Garry Wills, one of the most thoughtful Catholic intellectuals in the country and the author of many books including *Why I Am Catholic*. In response to a question about the long-term effects of the sex abuse scandal, Wills made this statement in the *Globe* on July 24:

> It's clear that there is something drastically wrong
> with the Catholic Church, and that is why what has
> happened in Boston and America is really a godsend,
> despite all the hurt, all the shame. [The abuse] was
> going on before, but now we know it's been going
> on, and now people are doing something about it.

There have been a whole series of statements from Vatican officials in the last few months saying, "The people in Boston who are critical of Cardinal Law are like Hitler, like Stalin, like [the Roman emperor] Decius, the persecutor of Christians"—all saying, "You cannot turn a priest over to civil authorities, you cannot submit to lay oversight of our actions."

What happened at Dallas [at the U.S. Conference of Catholic Bishops] really destroyed that. [The bishops] took very harsh stands: a very broad definition of sexual abuse, the turning over of every allegation [to civil authorities]. . . . That happened despite all these signals from Rome, saying, "Stand up to them; don't give in to the press." But [the bishops] knew how desperate things are. They said over and over, "The people won't put up with anything less." *They were looking to the people.* That is a huge change. [italics added]

We used to be told that a celibate priest cares more for you because he doesn't have the distractions of a wife and children. Who can think that now, with the pedophilia scandal? Would they have been less caring if they had had a wife to say, "You can't do this to children?" Or if a bishop had a son who had been raped? The old concepts of the priesthood are crumbling, and now more than ever the rate of

change is going to pick up. What happened in
Dallas is a good example: These are not guys who
were going to do any of that stuff before they were
forced to do it, and the reason they did it—despite
tremendous pressure from Rome not to do it—was
that the *people demanded it* . . . [italics added]
[Reprinted courtesy of *The Boston Globe*]

The Wills interview and other reports in the mainstream
media provided counterbalance to the relentless attacks on us
during August and into September: we were banned by bishops
in other dioceses; we were assaulted by national right-wing
Catholic media, and we were criticized by a small organization
called Faithful Voice that came into existence seemingly with
the sole purpose of attacking Voice of the Faithful! The group's
Web site states: "This site has been established to expose the
underpinnings of VOTF." Their main activity appears to be to
post on the site all the negative articles about Voice that they
can find.

—III—

While we had worked hard from the very beginning to make
sure our group would be welcoming to conservative Catholics,
the reality was that many conservatives were uncomfortable

with any movement that challenged the hierarchy *in any way*. And we were learning that there was particular concern among conservatives about our third goal, calling for structural change in the church. Since we had yet to precisely define what we meant by that, many conservatives viewed it as a threat to the existing structure of the church. In addition, our failure to specify what we meant by structural change gave those who misunderstood Voice an opportunity to define us in their own terms.

It was an opportunity that Deal Hudson, editor of *Crisis* magazine and one of the most outspoken Catholic conservative voices in the country, pursued with gusto. On August 8 he published a lengthy, scathing attack on our group. "Make no mistake, VOTF is a wolf in sheep's clothing," Hudson wrote. "And it's using this tragedy in our Church to advance its own political and theological agenda."

He attacked us on the basis of the beliefs held by some of the speakers at our convention—what he termed "radical views that are not in line with Church teaching." Hudson reserved particular scorn for Debra Haffner, an academic who had spoken at one of our convention breakout sessions on how to protect children from sexual predators. Hudson noted that Ms. Haffner was a member and former president of the Sexuality Information and Education Council of the United States (SIECUS). "SIECUS promotes guidelines for sex education for children grades K–12, guidelines which approve of children ages 5–8 being taught that masturbation and homosexuality are acceptable practices," he wrote in online commentary not long after the convention. "Not only that, they also urge that 12- to 15-year-olds be taught how to obtain and use contraceptives."

Hudson wrote that Thomas Groome, a professor of theology at Boston College, had been quoted as saying that priestly celibacy "has to be revisited, likewise the exclusion of women from ministry has to be rethought."

Hudson was sharply critical of a document on our Web site entitled "Discerning the Spirit: A Guide for Renewing and Restructuring the Catholic Church."

> The guide also relies heavily on the Vatican II document *Lumen Gentium* to support VOTF's push for a more "democratic" Catholic Church. It quotes the following passage in support of greater lay governance in the Church: "Thus every layman, by virtue of the very gifts bestowed upon him, is at the same time a witness and a living instrument of the mission of the Church herself" (LG §33). However, lay involvement is quite a different thing from the kind of "democratic" Church that VOTF so desperately wants. The establishment of a democratic Church was not the intent of Vatican II, as a later passage in *Lumen Gentium* explains: "The laity should

promptly accept in Christian obedience what is decided by the pastors who, as teachers and rulers of the Church, represent Christ" (LG §37). This kind of selective reading of Church documents can be dangerously misleading.

Just as we were being criticized by Deal Hudson and Faithful Voice, bishops on Long Island and in Connecticut banned Voice of the Faithful from meeting on church property within those dioceses. Pastors of a variety of churches—in Massachusetts, Maine, and elsewhere—had also passed the word through their parishes banning Voice groups from church property. Bishop William E. Lori of Bridgeport based his criticism on the *Pilot* complaint—he accused Voice of supporting We Are Church, the Germany-based Catholic reform group.

Attacks also continued in the media. An opinion article in the *Wall Street Journal* predicted that we would at some point advocate electing bishops and permitting married priests and women's ordination. Jim Post countered by saying that those attacking us "clearly have an agenda to cast doubt" on our integrity, but that the only label that accurately characterized our group was "Catholic."

Jim considered our group to be engaged in a life-and-death struggle. "There was nothing more important than responding to the attacks because they were targeted at the heart of the organization," he said. "If we didn't succeed in fighting back, we'd be out of business."

Jim was chatting in the office one evening with Ernie Corrigan, a veteran of many political wars.

"They're not just out to get you," Ernie agreed with Jim. "They're out to *crush* you."

— I V —

While all of this was happening, we were working internally to prepare a thoughtful response to the criticism. On August 20, a month to the day after the convention, we sent an e-mail to all twenty-two thousand Voice members in which we explained some things, clarified others, and generally defended our movement. We made clear that, as a group, "We accept the teaching authority of the church." We also made clear, "We do take the position that bishops fail in their role as shepherds and teachers when they refuse to engage the laity in a meaningful and substantive discussion of the issues."

In the e-mail, which was signed by Jim Post, we apologized for inviting Debra Haffner to speak because she was a "leader of several organizations that have taken positions at odds with the Catholic Church's teaching on abortion and sexuality."

Soon thereafter, Deal Hudson was back at us again, circulating his attack on the Internet. Hudson wrote:

To Jim Post and the leaders of VOTF, I say this:
You're known by the company you keep. If VOTF
wants to entertain the ideas of dissenting theologians and non-Catholics, that's its right. However, it
cannot then expect us to overlook these associations
when we're forming our opinions of the "mission"
of VOTF. I, for one, can't trust an organization that
claims to represent all Catholics but limits itself to
one ideological view. It would demonstrate far more
integrity for VOTF to simply acknowledge and de-
fend their liberal theological agenda.

This attack was inaccurate for two reasons. First, we did
not seek to limit ourselves to "one ideological view." We had invited conservatives to speak at our convention, but they declined to attend. Second, the argument of "guilt by association,"
if accepted, would limit full exploration of ideas.

Then, in September, we were asked to attend an organizing
meeting for a potential Voice chapter in Rockville Centre, Long
Island, where our group had been banned by Bishop William
Murphy, who had been called "Mansion Murphy" because of his
renovations. We went to the organizing meeting and found enormous enthusiasm. Several weeks later our group returned for an
open meeting and walked into a high school gymnasium over-
flowing with eight hundred people wanting to join the organization—and this in a diocese where we had already been banned!

Seeing this kind of response was immensely energizing. While the Long Island group was getting started, there were numerous other parish voices sprouting up around the country, a result in many cases of people who had come to our convention and returned home determined to get Voice started in their parish.

— V —

A critical weapon in the arsenal of those in the hierarchy who were attacking us was their vastly superior knowledge of canon law, the administrative code of the church, which they frequently cited. By September it was clear that we needed to know more about the rules that governed our church.

We therefore challenged the traditional belief that the hierarchy was the repository for all knowledge and that the laity, as supplicants, would simply accept the rules and ideas handed down to them. Again, the words of Garry Wills were wise and illuminating. He was asked by a journalist whether he thought the sexual abuse scandal would prompt Catholics to want to gain a deeper intellectual understanding of their church.

"Absolutely," he replied in a *Boston Globe* article.

People are asking for that, from history, from scripture, from tradition. It's not as hard as it was when all the documents were in Latin. There have been two tiers: a circle that was supposed to know those things, and the simple faithful who were not supposed to know. I remember visiting a church in Baltimore once, and saying to the priest, "I liked the visiting priest's sermon." He said, "Oh, he's a Jesuit; they like to tickle your ears with fancy things, but they don't feed the simple faith." The anti-intellectualism of the church has been a theme for many years.

At Voice, we needed to deepen our learning and we needed to do it quickly. Sister Evelyn Ronan at St. John's parish in Wellesley had a friend at Georgetown University who was a well-known canon lawyer. Ladislaus Orsy was into his eighties, a Jesuit of Hungarian birth who had been a young priest studying and teaching in Rome when Vatican II had convened there in the 1960s. Sister Evelyn contacted Father Orsy and he agreed to advise our group.

Father Orsy flew to Boston in mid-September for an all-day seminar with members of the steering committee. His presentation was lengthy and detailed but it was beautiful in its simplicity. He recalled the time of Vatican II as one of dramatic and historic change within the church, and he characterized that period as change from the "top down"—change initiated by the pope and passed down through cardinals and bishops and bestowed upon the laity. The essence of Vatican II, he said, was the involvement it envisioned from the laity, the empower-ment of the laity. Father Orsy said that under the dictates of Vatican II, the laity not only had a right to be involved with our church in a meaningful way; he confirmed that in times of crisis such as this one, we had a *responsibility* to bring the gifts and talents of the laity to bear to assist our church.

The education Father Orsy provided was referred to within the group as Orsy 101. "It was history and theology and canon law," said Jim Post. "He spoke in this soft, low voice with a slight accent reflecting his Hungarian heritage, telling us stories of Vatican II. He told us the laity was never more marginalized than today."

—⁂—

Our session with Father Orsy fortified us with the knowl-edge we needed to respond to attacks with intellectual pre-cision. Most important, it reinforced our belief that we had every right as Catholics to insist upon a place at the table; that we had every right to have a meaningful voice in church governance.

A deeper, more sustained intellectual initiative was getting under way at the same time as we were consulting Father Orsy. Boston College was inaugurating "The Church in the 21st Century," an effort to explore all aspects of the sex abuse crisis and other issues within the church. The program was designed as a two-year initiative focused on three issues: the relationship between lay people, priests, and the hierarchy; sexuality; and the transmission of faith to future generations.

In starting the effort, the president of Boston College, the Rev. William P. Leahy, a Jesuit, said something that was remarkably relevant to the attacks on our group. Father Leahy said that there would be no litmus tests applied to speakers or participants in the BC program. While we were being attacked largely on a guilt-by-association basis, the leader of one of the great Catholic universities in the world was saying something more expansive. "I don't think there are going to be any kinds of restrictions—people can pose the questions as they will," Father Leahy said in an interview with the *Globe*. "Some of the speakers we bring on campus may not reflect official church teaching, but that's how it is. By no means do I anticipate screening those who come on to campus. . . . And I have no difficulty if a bishop across the country or some local pastor may say that's not Catholic teaching—that's fine. We're trying to get at the large issues and stimulate thinking, encourage dialogue."

Father Leahy also characterized the BC project as an act of service to the church, not of dissent.

At the inaugural meeting of the BC conference, a crowd so large—more than four thousand people—showed up that the meeting had to be moved from a lecture hall into the hockey arena. Jack Connors, a prominent Catholic businessman and a BC trustee, delivered the keynote speech.

"I do not have the background or the training to distinguish between pedophilia and ephebophilia, but I do have the background to distinguish between right and wrong," he said. "The leadership of the archdiocese made a conscious decision to protect priests who were preying on innocent children over a period of many years."

Connors brought the crowd to its feet when he stated emphatically, "The church must change!"

But we were constantly reminded that change would come slowly, painfully—if at all. For there were forces within the church that would fiercely oppose *any* change.

—VI—

In early October a Massachusetts bishop announced that he was banning a Voice chapter from meeting on church property at St. Michael's parish in North Andover. Auxiliary Bishop Emilio Allue stated in a letter to the pastor of St. Michael's that "the activities and promotion of the Voice of the Faithful must be curtailed in order to avoid further scandal and polarity among our parishioners. For the sake of unity and Catholic orthodoxy in the parish, it is inappropriate to foster these meetings and to allow the members of the Voice of the Faithful to meet with the parish councils."

The Allue letter was the first time that anyone had put in writing that we were barred from using church property for our meetings. Some of our members initially reacted with sadness; for mainstream Catholics to whom the church is central to their lives, it is terribly hard to be in conflict with bishops. But the overriding emotion was anger—a powerful, visceral anger. In response to the news, one of our members exclaimed, "How dare they! How dare they ban us from our churches!"

As Jim Post put it, "Because we wanted our church to respond to the horrible deeds involved in the sex abuse scandal, the Boston hierarchy believed we should be kept out of churches?"

Bishop Allue had gone too far. Yet, as offensive as it was, the Allue letter was a gift of sorts—an opportunity. His banning called for more than a polite and deferential response. We consulted with Father Orsy and worked through a point-by-point rebuttal to his letter. Our letter to the bishop stated, "We believe your actions to be inconsistent with church teaching, Christian morality, the spirit of the Vatican II Council, and contrary to your pastoral duty." It continued,

> Voice of the Faithful is an organization of Catholic
> laity, properly formed as an association under the
> meaning of Canon 215 in the code of canon
> law. . . . Further, the teachings of the Second Vat-
> ican Council clearly articulate the right of the laity
> to form associations and set forth their obligation to
> make their voices heard on matters concerning the
> good of the Church. Voice of the Faithful was

formed to serve the Church by helping lay persons understand and address, individually and collectively, the most serious crisis in the 500-year history of the Catholic Church in North America: the perpetration and cover up by the hierarchy of sexual abuse of children by clergy. . . .

To my knowledge, you have not contacted anyone from Voice of the Faithful to inquire as to the truthfulness of the accusations lodged against us, nor to provide us any opportunity to respond. . . . There is no due process, no objective ascertainment of facts, no opportunity to hear the defendant and witnesses, no evidence produced, just the innuendo of "scandal" and "polarization," and a hint of heresy in the apparent lack of "orthodoxy."

These actions are devoid of principle, not in the spirit of the Vatican II Council, and lacking in Christian morality and basic justice when applied to a Catholic group that accepts the teaching authority of the Church. We might expect actions such as this from totalitarian rulers and repressive political regimes, but not from the stewards of our faith family. Bishop Allue, if you listen to slanderous accusations, fail to verify their veracity, and use unsubstantiated accusations as the justification for your public actions, you are either a participant in or a victim of an unbecoming smear campaign.

Bishop Allue, through innuendo and by implication, your letter defamed the good name of faithful Catholics in North Andover and elsewhere who, acting in collaboration as Voice of the Faithful, have wept for their Church, prayed for survivors and abusers alike, and struggled to find hope in the actions of Church leaders. Your actions in this matter are unfounded and unacceptable. Further, we believe the abrogation of due process in a matter of this nature constitutes a dereliction of pastoral duty. . . .

We pray that God may give you the grace to heal these wounds that afflict us all. Toward that end, we request that you rescind your instructions. . . . welcome Voice of the Faithful to parishes in the Merrimack region of the Archdiocese of Boston, and apologize to thousands of faithful Catholics who are members of Voice of the Faithful.

This forceful letter was a landmark document for Voice of the Faithful. Soon after we released it to the press, Cardinal Law met with a large number of parish priests to discuss the crisis. A number of them told him they believed that Voice was an organization comprised of good Catholics with the best intentions, and they urged him to lift the ban.

Amazingly, he did so. Just ten days after the Allue letter was issued, the Cardinal announced that part of the ban was rescinded; any existing Voice group could continue to meet on church property, although new groups would not be permitted to do so. This partial lifting of the ban was far from perfect. Certainly it was absurd that any new group would have to resort to meeting in a library or private home. But it was the first time all year that the hierarchy had yielded on *anything*. It was the first time we had fought back and won. And although it was a small victory, it gave our group immense confidence that we could fight the attacking hierarchy and win.

—VII—

In November the U.S. bishops planned to gather in Washington, D.C., to translate the charter they had developed back in Dallas into a set of rules. Between the Dallas meeting and the Washington event, however, the Vatican had gotten involved and weakened the charter the U.S. bishops had produced. In Dallas, the bishops had approved a policy of zero tolerance of sexual abuse; officials in Rome had said that approach was too harsh and could deny due process to accused priests. The Vatican directed that revisions be made. The bishops would vote on those revisions in Washington.

We decided to send a delegation to the Washington meeting to engage in dialogue with as many bishops as possible. We thought that we would be more successful than during the Dallas meeting due to our enhanced stature as an organization.

Our delegation to Washington included Steve Krueger, who by this time had become Voice's executive director, along with Mike Emerton, Svea Fraser, Mary Ann Keyes, and Susan Troy. In Washington, it was immediately clear that we faced a difficult challenge. Our group was confined to the lobby of the Hyatt, where the bishops rarely ventured. Their meetings were in a function room that was off-limits to us. When the bishops would come through the lobby we would make an attempt to chat with them, but that happened infrequently and our reception from most was chilly. The bishops issued press releases from the pressroom. Reporters would then come rushing to us and ask for our comment or for a more in-depth explanation. We were limited in our ability to comment because we didn't have any way of knowing what was going on inside the bishops' meeting and we had no advance notification of the content of their votes and statements. Thus we had no time to reflect before commenting to the press.

Steve Krueger, our executive director, thought the most sensible remedy for this problem would be to obtain copies of the press releases, review them carefully, and then answer questions from the press. Steve went through the lobby and made his way to the pressroom. He then had an experience that conjured all of the ugly, unpleasant memories of growing up Catholic in an inflexible parochial school.

"I'm ten steps over the threshold of the pressroom and I feel a hand come down hard on my shoulder, grabbing me," Steve recalled. He turned and saw that a nun who worked as a PR person for the bishops had physically grabbed him.

"'You have to leave,' she said. I told her who I was and she said, 'I know who you are. You have to leave.' It was as though I was an eight-year-old. I explained that I merely wanted to get copies of the press releases generated by the conference so that we could be better informed and better able to answer questions. She said I had to leave and that if I did not leave she would get hotel security. She could not have been more hostile."

Svea had a somewhat similar experience. She watched as the bishops—in black cassocks with pectoral crosses—would sometimes emerge from inside the confines of the hotel, generally moving rapidly past, intent on avoiding any contact with the laity. At one point Svea spotted Cardinal Law in the Hyatt lobby and went over to him and said a cordial hello, reminding the Cardinal who she was. He, of course, knew well who she was, for he had been the one who had paved the way for Svea to enroll at Blessed John XXIII Seminary in Weston. She told the Cardinal that she was "here with Voice of the Faithful and we wanted to be part of the solution." Cardinal Law responded by saying: "Svea, you know there are a lot of things lay people can do in the parishes."

And he was gone.

This was immensely frustrating to all of us. Susan Troy had difficulty fathoming why it was that the hierarchy seemed so frightened of us. "We were their best friends," she said. "We're not the hundreds of thousands who had already *left* the church. We were their best friends and they couldn't even see that. We're the most active members of the church, the Eucharistic Ministers, pastoral associates, parish council, lay ministers. *And we're frightening to them.* Wow!"

She wanted to say to the bishops, "You should not be pushing us away but embracing us and listening. Why are you threatened by faithful Catholics getting together and talking about healing the church? At the convocation back in March, Cardinal Law had said, 'We need to heal.' Okay, we'll help."

Susan found the bishop's conference "extremely sad, depressing, discouraging." She was deeply disappointed that the meeting was closed with no provision for access to the laity. "The night of the survivors' vigil, we hung around the lobby hoping to be able to interact with our bishops, our shepherds," she said. "It was ludicrous, bizarre. . . . Bishops would walk by and actively not make eye contact."

On Monday evening the many survivors who had gathered for the conference were holding a solidarity march and prayer service. A number of Voice members joined the march and prayer vigil at the church on Capitol Hill. Svea and Mary Ann Keyes had planned on doing so as well, but in the early evening they were standing out in front of the Hyatt when a caravan of empty buses pulled up to the front entrance. They watched as bishops filed out the front door of the Hyatt and boarded the buses. Svea heard someone say they were going to the basilica for mass.

"So the bishops were going to mass and the victims were going someplace else," Svea recalled. She thought everyone should be going to mass together. Svea and Mary Ann decided to look for a ride to the mass. One of the women working with the bishops promised to get them on one of the buses, but then the woman noted Svea's Voice badge and said she was sorry but that they would not be able to ride the buses. A few minutes later, though, as the convoy of buses was headed out, the woman apparently felt bad about leaving them out and she brought them over to a limousine idling by the curb. The limo, assigned to the bishops' conference, had gone unused and the woman urged Svea and Mary Ann to hop in.

They rode to the cathedral where they watched as 237 bishops, all of whom were now dressed in white, miters atop their heads, filed solemnly into the sanctuary. Svea sat, watching the bishops shuffle slowly along, listening to the strains of the organ, and hearing the muffle of a few protesters outside. She prayed, "God, please help us get it together. Help us hear what's outside."

When the mass was over, Svea and Mary Ann went outside and were surprised to see that the limousine which brought them was being used by a bishop. Their ride was gone. One of the chauffeurs noticed that they were stranded and he led them to the last of the buses and urged them to get on. With no other option available, they climbed aboard the bus— and saw that it was filled with bishops. There was one available seat—all the way in the rear. Slowly, they proceeded down the center aisle, past row after row after row of bishops. Svea and Mary Ann were greeted with silence. "No one spoke to us," Svea said. "Not a word." They sat in the back, initially unaware that they were adjacent to both Cardinal Egan of New York and Cardinal George of Chicago.

When the bus reached the Hyatt and everyone had disembarked, Svea tried to engage Cardinal George in conversation. She said she was a member of Voice of the Faithful and wanted to be part of the process of healing the church.

"You're dissidents," he replied to Svea—the "church lady;" a graduate of Blessed John XXIII Seminary, holder of a master's of divinity degree, a woman whose life was centered on her profound commitment to the Roman Catholic Church.

"What makes you say that?" Svea asked.

"Because of the people you have come and speak to you," he replied.

The collective behavior of the group of bishops was difficult to comprehend. Our executive director getting grabbed and thrown out of a function room for wanting a press release; bishops refusing to meet with survivors; cardinals sitting on a bus refusing to speak to two good Catholic women because they represented Voice of the Faithful.

"Jesus Christ would have been with the victims," Svea thought. "The shepherds of the church don't know their flock."

We were confined to the hotel lobby until the last day, when we were kicked out of the hotel completely and forced out onto the sidewalk out front. Had we been avowed enemies of Catholicism, we could not have been treated with greater disdain.

CHAPTER 1 1

THE CARDINAL RESIGNS
BUT THE CHALLENGE
PERSISTS

— I —

IN LATE OCTOBER 2002, after ten months of conflict with survivors, laity, and his own priests, Cardinal Law mounted a public relations campaign that included meetings with large groups of clergy and separate gatherings with survivors. During a session with about four hundred priests held in Arlington, a Boston suburb, the cardinal was urged by a number of priests to take a more open and positive approach toward Voice of the Faithful.

Days later, the Cardinal held a meeting with about seventy-five survivors—as well as some members of Voice—in the basement of St. Francis Church in the town of Dracut, Massachusetts. Victims cried as they related the details of their stories. "I beg your forgiveness . . ." the Cardinal said. "I have the pain of someone who made terrible mistakes and caused you pain."

Soon after the meeting in Dracut, the Cardinal stood at the altar of Holy Cross Cathedral in Boston and in an emotional statement said, "I did assign priests who had committed sexual abuse. . . . I acknowledge my own responsibility for decisions which led to intense suffering. While that suffering was never intended, it could have been avoided, had I acted differently."

As reporter Michael Paulson put it in the *Boston Globe*, "After nearly 10 months of ducking public appearances, failing to answer letters and calls, entering buildings through side doors, and seeming to disappear for days, Law . . . has haltingly reemerged into the public glare. And after months of apologies that never seemed to sink in, over the last two weeks he has added a degree of human contact that has made his familiar expressions of sorrow and humility seem, to the unhappy priests, angry victims, and restive laypeople he has met with, more believable."

I had no doubt the Cardinal was sincere in his apologies. And I was gratified that he was making an effort, for it was critically important that he humble himself before survivors and that he convey the message to all Catholics that he was genuinely remorseful for what he had done. But I remained concerned about the excessive focus on Cardinal Law as *the* problem.

Meanwhile, Voice of the Faithful continued our efforts to meet with Cardinal Law. We were pleased that he finally agreed to a meeting—surely part of his PR initiative—and the session was scheduled for November 26, two days before Thanksgiving.

While we hoped for a positive meeting, the new, contrite, and accommodating Cardinal seen in public was not the one who addressed our group in private. After a prayer and a brief exchange of greetings, Cardinal Law launched into a lengthy oration on the crisis in a tone that was surprisingly aggressive. At one juncture he spoke about the 1993 church policy on abuse that called for removing priests against whom credible allegations had been made. He pointed at Jim Post in an assertive way and demanded to know whether Jim knew how many abuse cases there had been since the policy was put in place. (Jim, in fact, *did* know.) Later in the meeting, Steve Krueger respectfully disagreed with the Cardinal on a point, and Law, in a hostile tone, said sharply, "Steve, you *know* that's not so."

It was an outburst of emotion and annoyance that someone would challenge him, said Jim. "He was annoyed that lay people were challenging him."

During the meeting, Jim, who led our delegation, clearly enunciated our core message: that we are Catholics who love our church and that we are determined to make a difference. When Jim indicated that Voice wanted to be helpful, Law replied that he did not want or need help from such a group. The Cardinal repeatedly said he had questions, particularly concerning our goal of seeking structural change within the church. At the end of the meeting we agreed to have our theologian meet with a theologian from the archdiocese to discuss the change issue in detail. But our delegation left with the overriding sense that the Cardinal had been unwelcoming.

—⁓—

Days later, in the first week of December, more evidence of shocking misconduct by the Cardinal became public. Specific actions by the Cardinal were revealed in twenty-two hundred pages of long-buried archdiocesan documents that were released by plaintiff attorneys in the lawsuits against the archdiocese. Boston Catholics who had thought the scandal could get no worse were shocked anew as the documents revealed how sexually abusive priests were routinely transferred to new parishes where no one was told of their past history. The documents revealed a depth of depravity among some priests that was astounding. As Voice executive director Steve Krueger put it: "The revelations exceeded anything that could have been imagined."

There was the case of Father Robert Meffan, a Massachusetts priest who had sexually abused high school girls who were preparing to become nuns. The priest presented himself as the second coming of Christ and said that he wanted the girls to be "brides of Christ." Meffan told the *Globe* that he was "trying to get them to love Christ even more intimately and even more closely. . . . They were wonderful girls."

Father Thomas Forry of South Weymouth was accused of having a lengthy sexual relationship with a woman. Her former husband accused Forry of assaulting and molesting their son as well. Forry's response was to threaten to have the man killed. Forry would later admit to having a ten-year relationship with a woman. Cardinal Law sent Forry back to his parish.

There was the case of Father James Foley, who fathered two children. The woman with whom he was sexually involved later died of a drug overdose after going to bed with the priest. Foley had also allegedly had sexual affairs in other assignments. Nonetheless, Law kept him in active ministry.

There was the case of a priest who had given drugs to minors in return for sex.

David Clohessy, national director of the Survivors Network of those Abused by Priests, said, "It is very clear from the documents that Cardinal Law and top diocesan officials knew far more, far earlier, about far more priests and their abusive behavior than officials have ever let on, but did so very little to protect not just innocent children, but adults, boys and girls, church employees, and regular lay people."

The response to the release of documents was a new level of anguish, a new level of heartache and fury. Now there seemed no question that the Cardinal would have to go. A few days after the revelations, Law traveled to Rome.

Soon thereafter, a remarkable voice was heard: fifty-eight priests in the Archdiocese of Boston signed a letter urging Law to resign. The priests, led by the members of the Boston Priest's Forum with whom we had met earlier, wrote: "While this is obviously a difficult request, we believe in our hearts that this is a necessary step that must be taken if healing is to come to the archdiocese. The priests and people of Boston have lost confidence in you as their spiritual leader."

Such a statement from parish priests was a rare event within the Catholic Church—an uprising, a courageous rebellion among priests whose jobs and pensions were at risk if they alienated the Cardinal. I thought back to the sweltering evening we had met with the leaders of the Boston Priest's Forum and considered how blessed we were have men such as these in our parishes as our spiritual guides and partners. Father Bob Bullock, who had been at our meeting, told the press that the "letter was done with great pain and great thought, but also with a sense of responsibility to the situation in which we're involved. To come to this point is very, very painful."

It was now essential that the meeting of our Voice representative council revisit the issue of the Cardinal's resignation. Unlike our raucous debate many months earlier, this discussion was somber, the outcome preordained. As the votes for resignation were counted, I noted that several of the brave individuals who had supported the Cardinal in our earlier vote had now become convinced that he must go. I felt a great satisfaction that our democracy of the laity was functioning as we had hoped it would. But as David Castaldi stated so well, it was not a time to celebrate. It was a time of sadness that such abuses had occurred and that a call for resignation was required. On the following day, the *Globe* carried pictures of the Voice councilors standing solemnly as their votes for the resignation of their cardinal were counted.

Two days after our vote, on December 13, 2002, Cardinal Law met at the Vatican with Pope John Paul II. The Cardinal offered his resignation, and the Holy Father accepted.

— I I —

The first casualty of the sex abuse scandal had been trust. The second was money. In the immediate wake of the scandal, donations to the church plummeted, causing drastic cutbacks in an array of important educational and social programs.

We had established the Voice of Compassion fund to help address this problem. Cardinal Law had been offered the funds—$56,000. Under the terms of our proposal, the archdiocese had a certain amount of time to decide whether to accept the gift. Since no decision was made by the deadline, December 9, just a few days before the Cardinal's resignation, we carried out our plan to offer the money to Catholic Charities, one of the largest and most effective social service agencies in the area. The group, whose board members had been appointed by the Cardinal, accepted our donation. This was seen by some as an act of defiance, but Peter Meade, vice chairman of Catholic Charities, said he saw it rather as an "act of wisdom." He said the money would go into a fund to pay for food, clothes, and toys for poor families at Christmas. Donations to the Cardinal's appeal had fallen so sharply that these needy individuals were secondary victims of the abuse crisis.

The day after the board said it would accept the funds, however, Bishop Edyvean, who became the temporary leader of the archdiocese following the resignation, publicly expressed his displeasure with the decision. "The acceptance on the part of Catholic Charities of a sum of money raised by Voice of the Faithful was done without the agreement of the Archdiocese of Boston. The earlier restriction which Cardinal Law had placed on receiving these monies had not been rescinded at the time of this action, nor has it been at this time."

The bishop's remarks reminded me of our meeting in the spring when Father O'Connell had angrily lectured us about the exclusive right of the bishop to raise such money. I recalled the embarrassing moment where Father O'Connell had lowered his hand and referred to money for the poor, then raised his hand high and talked of principle. Bishop Edyvean had seemed embarrassed by Father O'Connell's tirade at the time, but now, sadly, Edyvean was confirming that he too put the power of the hierarchy above the collection of money for the poor. And Bishop Edyvean was now demonstrating, as we expected, that even though Cardinal Law had gone, nothing really had changed.

These discussions about our contribution occurred in the context of a broader financial crisis in the Boston archdiocese. These problems became a major concern of the interim administrator for the archdiocese, Bishop Richard G. Lennon, whom the Pope appointed to replace Cardinal Law. Bishop Lennon said early in 2003 that the financial shortfall would require closing some Catholic schools and cutting back on a wide variety of social services to the poor.

At this point additional funds had accumulated in the Voice of Compassion fund and they were offered to Bishop Lennon, as funds had previously been offered to Cardinal Law. The offerings were beginning to serve as a litmus test for the willingness of the hierarchy to work with Voice. Since Bishop Lennon had refused to meet with us, or lift the ban on formation of new Voice affiliates that Law had initiated, we were not surprised when he announced in late March that he would *not* accept the donation from our group. More than that, he said that he would not permit Catholic Charities to accept the funds either. The bishop's spokesman told the press: "Bishop Lennon stated that it is his firm belief that you cannot separate the charitable works of the church from the office of the bishop. Catholic Charities has been directed not to accept the money, and all the other entities of the archdiocese are also being informed of that directive as well."

Peter Meade of Catholic Charities was quoted in the *Globe* saying, "The board's position has been very clear—we are continuing a hundred-year-long position of accepting money from those who contribute, and it would be profoundly sad if we had to revisit this issue. This isn't about power or politics, but about feeding the hungry and clothing the naked."

Neal Finnegan, chairman of the Catholic Charities board, told the paper: "We have been put in a difficult position by these events, but we felt that we had a higher responsibility to the needs of the poor, and to the basic mission of Catholic Charities."

Fortunately, the courage of people like Peter Meade and Neal Finnegan and many other members of the Catholic Charities board was unflinching. In spite of Bishop Lennon's directive not to accept the funds, the board voted overwhelmingly to accept the money. While there had been rumors that the bishop would fire the board if they defied him, he did not do so.

Steve Pope, the Boston College theologian, put it well, saying that the conflict between the Catholic Charities board and the bishop "continues the erosion of the unity of the church, and shows how deep the dissatisfaction is with the leadership, and it will certainly concern other bishops around the country. I don't think this means the people who voted to take the money are being disloyal as Catholics, but I do think they believe that part of being Catholic is acting the way Jesus did, which is by being concerned for the poor, and putting that above the public show of unanimity."

—III—

While Cardinal Law and his colleagues in the Boston hierarchy were opposed to Voice of the Faithful, the responses of bishops throughout the country were varied. In some places we were banned arbitrarily, and in others there was an excellent dialogue in progress; in most there was indifference and a wary skepticism about our stated goal of changing the church.

During the summer of 2003, I had the opportunity to meet with the leaders of three different archdioceses. After an exchange of letters, I met with Cardinal Eugene George in Chicago. He was cordial and open-minded throughout. We discussed his thesis work on Father Teilhard de Chardin, whom I greatly admire. Regarding the current situation of Catholicism, George said he believed that there was a "crisis" in the church independent of the sexual abuse scandal, as indicated by the fall in vocations and attendance at mass. He attributed much of the problem to American secular society.

I had been encouraged that he had written in his letter, "the move to increase lay participation in church governance [is] . . . a goal that deserves to be encouraged." But he said that our motto, "Keep the Faith, Change the Church," was problematic, and that any change in the church, unless most carefully thought out, would change the faith. I said we did not want to change the basic doctrines but that we wanted a means for the *sensus fidelium* to be refined and discussed in communion with the hierarchy. He suggested that "Keep the Faith, Change the Way the Church Acts" might not cause as much concern.

My meeting with Archbishop Daniel Buechlein of Indianapolis was nostalgic for me because the chancery is located in what was my high school—Cathedral High—and the Archbishop's impressive office had been my spartan classroom forty-five years earlier. Archbishop Buechlein is also a close friend of my father's. We reviewed a brochure about Voice that I had brought and he took note of this quotation from Saint Cyprian, bishop of Carthage, circa A.D. 248: "I have made it a rule, ever since the beginning of my episcopate, to make no decision merely on the strength of my own personal opinion without consulting you [priests and deacons], and without the approbation of the people." Archbishop Buechlein said that he agreed with the statement, and worked closely with the laity as Saint Cyprian advocated. He said that without lay support his job would be impossible.

Like Cardinal George, Archbishop Buechlein expressed concern over our goal of changing the church. I explained that we did not seek to change core doctrine, although I added that it might be difficult to draw a distinction between "core" and changeable positions of the church. He said it was not difficult at all—that the teachings of the church were clear, contained in the new Catechism on his desk. We did not pursue the topic further, but I suspect that had we done so we would have disagreed about what is open to discussion.

As I left, I said there was something I needed to tell him about the glass award he had given me as an alumnus for "Celebrating Catholic School Values."

"I know," he said. "You wanted to smash it. I read your speech to the convention on the VOTF Web site." He graciously accepted my explanation that my anger was directed at the debasement of those values that had occurred and not at the award—which still stands on my desk.

In Cincinnati I met with Archbishop Daniel Pilarczyk, a distinguished church leader who formerly served as president of the U.S. Catholic Conference of Bishops, and who had worked with Cardinal Bernardin for many years. Archbishop Pilarczyk had met previously with Jim Post and thus had a favorable impression of our organization. He reaffirmed that he is "satisfied that there is nothing contrary to Church teaching in the work of VOTF." He said that he views Voice as an "association of lay faithful [that] . . . has the good of the Church at heart." He agreed to meet with representatives of our group in the future to continue our dialogue.

While I did not have the chance to visit him, the Most Rev. John McCarthy, bishop emeritus of the Austin (Texas) diocese, sent a very encouraging letter to Voice in which he stated that "our church has many problems but structurally one of the most serious is in my opinion the absence of the means to bring about orderly change when it is needed."

There were other positive developments in 2003 that gave us reason to hope. One was the appointment of Father Sean O'Malley as bishop of Boston. Bishop Sean, as he prefers to be called, was selected in early July to replace Bishop Lennon.

Bishop Sean immediately changed the tone of the hierarchy in Boston. "People are more important than money," he said on his very first day in his new position, and it was clear he meant it. He was a humble man, a Capuchin friar who wears a simple brown robe, a man seen in previous assignments as a people's bishop. I was quoted in the *New York Times* as saying that his appointment by the Pope was an inspired choice.

With both a master's degree in religious education and a doctorate in Spanish and Portuguese literature, Father O'Malley is a man of great intellect. He carries himself in a softly spoken, humble manner, yet he can be firm and direct as a leader. He was so effective in his work early on in Washington, D.C., where he focused on housing for the poor and working with needy immigrants, that he was named a bishop before age forty. From the mid-1980s until 1992 he served as bishop in St. Thomas in the Virgin Islands, where he founded soup kitchens, homeless shelters, and a program for pregnant teenagers.

After a terrible sexual abuse scandal in Fall River, Massachusetts, Bishop O'Malley was brought in and restored dignity to the diocese as he forged a financial settlement with victims.

O'Malley was so successful in Fall River that when a sexual abuse scandal struck Palm Beach, Florida, he was sent down there where he performed with the same degree of compassion and leadership, bringing healing to that diocese as well.

And so Bishop O'Malley seemed an excellent choice to begin the healing process in Boston. He promised to settle the hundreds of sex abuse lawsuits against the archdiocese, and he went to work doing just that. Within a matter of months, in large measure due to his own personal involvement at the negotiating table with plaintiff lawyers, he struck a settlement deal: $85 million for 552 plaintiffs.

We were deeply gratified that the settlement helped provide a sense of closure and justice for many survivors. There had been moments when some survivors—certainly Art Austin at our convention—expressed the view that Voice was too mainstream, too timid; that we did not stand up assertively enough for survivors. But the truth is that we have never lost sight of the brave witness of survivors that gave birth to our organization and our efforts on their behalf have clearly had an impact. There is no stronger proof of that than the words of David Clohessy, national director of SNAP: "I've been at this 12 years, and I vividly recall when every letter we got from a Catholic layperson was hostile, but now the supportive letters outnumber the hostile ones 40 or 50 to one. [Voice of the Faithful] helped create the climate that enables victims to come forward and break their silence, and the value of that is incalculable."

But the enduring test for our organization would come *after* the settlement. On September 9, 2003, when the settlement was announced, we issued a statement saying the laity "must insist that real reforms now take place and that the culture that allowed such abuse to occur and to be concealed [must] be transformed into one that operates openly and honestly." Our statement warned that it "would be an enormous mistake for anyone to celebrate or believe that things can return to . . . business as usual. . . . The settlement, while an important substantive and symbolic step forward, is but one step on a road that stretches before us."

The next milestone on the road before us came on November 9, 2003, when Archbishop O'Malley met with a delegation of Voice members led by Jim Post. In the meeting the Archbishop said it was a time for healing and reconciliation, and he agreed to review the prior refusals of Cardinal Law and Bishop Lennon to accept money from Voice or to permit us to form new affiliates. After the meeting, his spokesperson, Father Coyne, was quoted in the *Globe* by Michael Paulson as saying "each member of Voice who came made it very clear . . . that they are faithful, good members of their parishes and that the people who are part of Voice are not dissidents, people who are not out to spread disunity within the church but just people who want to help the church move forward. . . . All of us around the table did not see divisions between Catholic and Catholic, but mainly just saw some issues within the family that need to be resolved."

We were pleased by this accurate portrayal of Voice by Father Coyne. However, when he was attacked on the following day by Deal Hudson, Father Coyne retreated to the position that he was just repeating what the Voice members had told him. Nonetheless, it was clear that Archbishop O'Malley had set a new tone that we believe holds much promise.

Another positive step—perhaps half-step would be more accurate—came quite unexpectedly in the late fall of 2003. I was getting my hair cut when Joe, my barber, asked about the book. I told him it starts out with a difficult encounter in the Boston chancery with two members of the hierarchy—which brought to mind the obstinance of Bishop Edyvean and, in particular, young Father O'Connell.

As I paid for the haircut and prepared to leave, a man in his thirties entered the shop and smiled pleasantly at me. "Hello, Dr. Muller. Nice to see you," he said warmly. When I wasn't immediately able to place him, he added, "Father Mark O'Connell. We met at the chancery last year."

I was struck by the contrast between his pleasant demeanor now and the harsh statements he had made to us across the boardroom table—the only time I had ever seen him before. As Joe prepared to cut his hair, I asked, "Father, would you have a few minutes to talk when you're finished?"

"Certainly," he replied.

When Joe finished, Father O'Connell and I walked over to Johnny's Diner in Newton Center. Sitting on opposite sides of the small Formica table, we both ordered hot chocolate.

"Father," I said, "thank you for introducing yourself to me, and for this opportunity to talk. The book starts with our difficult exchange in the chancery. I reported all of your words, which those of us who were there felt were harsh, and now, after your pleasant greeting, I was hoping for a more positive exchange. Reconciliation is an important part of the Catholic tradition."

"Yes," he said. Then he added, "Things are better."

"Why are they better?" I asked.

"Because of Archbishop O'Malley and the progress he has made with the entire issue. He has reached settlements with the survivors. Just today he announced that he would sell the Cardinal's residence. And, although I cannot speak for the chancery now, I know he is in a productive dialogue with Voice."

I told Father O'Connell that we were pleased with the dialogue with Archbishop O'Malley, and that we were very pleased by the statement of Father Coyne that Voice members were loyal Catholics and that this was a dispute within the family.

We talked about the unpleasant encounter at the chancery during the meeting with Bishop Edyvean. Father O'Connell's views as expressed that day remained unchanged.

I pressed him on whether he had any positive thoughts about Voice, and he granted that some dialogue is better than none.

"Yes," he said. "It's good that we're having chocolate together and talking."

As we left Johnny's, we spoke of the importance of the

church in our lives and learned that we both had uncles and aunts in the clergy. As we parted, I expressed my amazement at the coincidence of our meeting, and asked jokingly if perhaps the Holy Spirit had arranged our schedules.

He smiled, and we both wondered.

Though that road is a long one, we are determined to stay the course.

—IV—

One of the genuinely remarkable things about Voice of the Faithful is that our core group from the earliest days has remained active in the organization. When I think back to that first Sunday after mass, the day when our group came together, I recall the faces in the pews: Jim Post, who is now president of Voice, a tireless leader and articulate spokesman; Mary Scanlon, head of the Survivor Support Working Group; Peggie Thorp, editor of our online newsletter, *In the Vineyard*, and our quarterly publication, *Voice*; Susan Troy, leader of Prayerful Voice; Luise Dittrich, the lead press person for our national organization; and Scott Fraser, our treasurer. Paul Baier is involved at certain times, though he has started a new organization dedicated to survivors called Survivors First (www.SurvivorsFirst.org). Other early pioneers—Steve Krueger, Mary Ann Keyes, David Castaldi, Andrea Johnson, Kathi Aldridge, Maura O'Brien, Margaret Roylance, Bill and Cathy Fallon—have not only remained active but continue to play major roles within the movement.

For us to have the impact we have had so far has required the perseverance and determination of thousands of Voice members. "We didn't anticipate the stonewalling and other tactics bishops used to avoid relating to laity," observed Luise Dittrich. "We assumed they would be so contrite and so shamed they would be accountable, because that's what happens in the world—accountability happens." But real-world accountability—the kind that exists in business or politics, for example—has not yet reached the bishops, and so we keep the pressure on. The hierarchy must know that we will only get stronger. While some bishops have chosen to work with us, most have not, and some are openly hostile. As Luise put it, "Instead of reaching out in a pastoral way, they're counting on us beating our heads against the wall until we fall down exhausted."

While they cannot identify a basis to oppose us in canon law, individual bishops continue to obstruct our efforts. When we were planning our conference at Fordham University in New York in October 2003, for example, we prepared an advertisement to run in Catholic newspapers announcing the event and inviting all to attend. This was a conference at which Catholics would gather to pray, listen to Catholic speakers, including priests, and then join together for a liturgy.

Yet all five Catholic newspapers we approached refused to run our ad. Catholic newspapers in the archdiocese of New

York, the diocese of Brooklyn, as well as New Jersey dioceses in Metuchen, Paterson, and Trenton refused to print our ads about the conference. "We offered to alter our ad in any way in order to meet whatever objections they had," said Marie Ford Reilly, the coordinator of the conference. "We were never told what their specific objections were. They just kept turning us down."

In spite of the advertising ban, our conference sold out, attracting fifteen hundred Catholics from around the country. The focus of the conference was on how lay people can work in cooperation with clergy and the hierarchy in renewing the church. The real message was one of hope—that working together we can take the church to a better place.

While we may have lost our innocence and our naïveté, we have not lost our leadership or our determination to see the job through. For every setback there is a triumph that sustains us, such as the success of the Fordham conference. We know that we have already accomplished a great deal. We have made steady progress on our first two goals—supporting survivors and priests of integrity. It is our third goal—creating structural change within the church—that is the most complex and controversial, yet here we have progressed as well.

"We have provided a forum for people to stand up and speak their mind," Svea asserted. "Our biggest challenge is to persevere, to not give up, to continue to support each other in our commitment to healing the church. The fact that all these good people are committed to this gives me hope."

One thing we know for sure is that the traditional model of having the docile laity "pray, pay, and obey" has led to a church in decline and created the circumstances in which the sexual abuse scandal could occur. Scott Appleby, the Notre Dame theologian, has urged that Catholics "stay, pray, and inveigh," so that a better church might be created. Voice is the obvious channel through which effective inveighing might take place.

— V —

A critical step in creating a democracy for the laity has been the establishment of the Voice Governing Council, the deliberative body that has ultimate responsibility for Voice. At the end of 2003, the council was composed of approximately two hundred members who represent the various Voice constituencies. Most councilors have been selected by their local affiliate, while some occupy at-large positions created to retain the valuable perspective of the original cofounders. The council meets bimonthly in Boston and follows rules similar to those used by a city or town council. Maura O'Brien and Frances O'Leary brought their prior experience with town government to the task of serving as moderators of the council.

The first major issue addressed by the council was a reconsideration of the call for the resignation of Cardinal Law in December of 2002. While the media reports focused on the outcome of the vote—the call for his resignation—I thought that the more important news was that a representative group of lay Catholics was using democracy to express its views for governance of the church.

Critics of Voice accused us of being a Trojan horse in which the reformers would pursue their hidden agenda of advocacy for women priests and other divisive issues. However, the true nature of the council was revealed in its first major document. Under the leadership of Margaret Roylance, the council developed a thoughtful document on structural change whose main emphasis was on the establishment and proper functioning of parish and diocesan committees authorized by Vatican II. Bishop Daily of Brooklyn, who had once banned Voice, studied this document and others from the Voice Governing Council and reversed his ban, stating that the actions of Voice were not contrary to church teachings.

The council has also helped move Voice from a Boston-based to a national organization. Voice national headquarters in Newton, Massachusetts, houses a talented staff of more than forty underpaid and unpaid volunteers, in a thriving nerve center. The eventual plan is to create an international council that will be composed of representatives of the various national groups.

In addition to its deliberative function, the council has elected a slate of officers and established an executive office. This important business infrastructure, which is essential to sustain the growth of Voice, has been made possible by more than

$600,000 that has been donated by Catholics eager to strengthen their church. Among other things, the money helps Voice reach a virtual community of thousands through its excellent Web site, www.votf.org, which contains a complete listing of Voice affiliates.

— VI —

Voice of the Faithful faces several major hurdles in the years ahead. One internal threat is the likelihood that our devoted and overworked staff will not be able to sustain their pace without an increase in pay to near-market levels. At present most workers are volunteers; paid staff receive wages that are approximately half of what they would receive for similar work in other organizations. Another factor that threatens staff morale and the effectiveness of thousands of volunteers is potential burnout. Many of our members have worked at unsustainable levels and must be relieved by others as they lower their work for Voice to levels that can be maintained. Much of the energy that has gone into Voice is sustained by hope—if volunteers do not see continued progress, despair will ensue, and the organization will falter. One of our biggest hurdles in the years to come will be raising the very substantial financial resources needed to sustain a truly effective effort.

In addition to these internal threats we also expect external difficulties. The greatest of these is the possibility that Catholicism will take a narrow view of the sexual abuse scandal and treat this symptom without addressing the underlying disease.

Another external threat is the abandonment of Catholicism by those who could be most helpful to Voice. There are many talented individuals who have already left or are considering leaving the Catholic Church. Many have left because of the abuse scandal. It is precisely these individuals, who care enough about morality and religion to demand high standards for their church, who could play a role in building Voice. If they leave the church in substantial numbers instead of banding together to change it, the prospects for Voice—and the Catholic Church—will be diminished.

—∞—

At the heart of our strategy to change the church is the expansion of our Parish Voice program. In 2003 we voted additional resources to this effort to organize in parishes, which are the unit of greatest importance to most Catholics. The idea of Parish Voice is to bring our group to the parish so that Catholics "can begin fulfilling the Voice mission and goals at the local level with family and friends. It's in our parishes that we will foster basic lay involvement in the guidance and governance of the church. And it's in our communities that we can most immediately help the survivors of sexual abuse by priests, support priests of integrity, and work for structural change within our beloved Catholic Church."

During 2003 we doubled the number of Parish Voice affiliates to 190 throughout the United States, Canada, Australia, and New Zealand. Our goal is to build an effective Parish Voice affiliate in every diocese in the United States and then every diocese throughout the world. Under the visionary leadership of Mary Ann Keyes, the Parish Voice program has become the source of our growing strength and hundreds more Parish Voice affiliates are currently in the planning stages. In addition to the Parish Voice affiliate strategy, we will continue our effort to enroll supporters via the Internet and e-mail.

With Parish Voice and our Internet strategy, we are building our organization from the ground up to reflect the will of the people in the most fundamentally democratic way possible. When it is large enough, most of the hierarchy will find it a valuable partner, and those who oppose it will find it difficult to ignore or destroy.

— V I I —

As I look back upon the journey of Voice of the Faithful, I am amazed by both the obstacles we have faced and the progress we have made. I agree completely with Svea that it is the commitment to Voice of so many good people that gives me hope. I'm also confident that a series of forces now converging will foster the changes in Catholicism that Voice seeks. These forces include the tradition of Catholicism to change with history, a global trend toward democratization, the mandates of Vatican II, the determination of the laity, and the Internet.

The historical backdrop of the church, taking the long view, is encouraging. Throughout its two-thousand-year history, the church has changed significantly and in many positive ways. Even organizations whose cultures are deeply resistant to change do evolve over time, and the church is no exception. The global trend toward democratization and transparency will work against the secrecy and concentration of power that enabled the sex abuse scandal to occur. And democracy is already embedded in parts of the church. Cardinals vote for the pope; bishops discuss resolutions, hold debates, and vote. A democratic and collaborative voice for the faithful could be immensely helpful to the hierarchy. It could assist the church in adapting the message of Christ so that it may be more readily accepted in the twenty-first century. In a poll conducted by the *Globe* in 2003, 52 percent of respondents said that modernizing church attitudes on social issues would bring them closer to Catholicism. While some would equate "modernizing" with capitulation to secular decadence, there are many deeply moral and spiritual individuals who seek changes that would not alter the faith, or conflict with the teachings of Christ. Voice would be an ideal group to identify issues of importance to Catholics for discussion and then help facilitate the dialogue.

For an organization dependent upon the confidence and devotion of its members to militantly resist the powerful force of democracy is a perilous course. It is particularly perilous when the church's own mandates from Vatican II call for more openness and a greater role for the laity. Given the immensely powerful global trends and the mandates of Vatican II, lay people are determined to force change.

Finally, the World Wide Web has provided the laity with an extraordinary means to exert their influence in the church in a revolutionary manner unavailable to prior generations. The Internet has made possible the creation and rapid growth of Voice of the Faithful. As we organized, we were in hourly communication with one another via e-mail even as the media spread news of our efforts worldwide. The Web permitted a scattered, grassroots movement to take collective action.

While the optical cables and photonic switches of the Internet are new, the concept of a beneficial, rising global consciousness that would aid spirituality was articulated more than eighty years ago by the Jesuit anthropologist Pierre Teilhard de Chardin (1881–1955). I read his brilliant book *The Phenomenon of Man* in college and have been guided in my scientific work by his visionary ideas. He wrote of the origin of the earth as a mass of chemicals, some of which evolved into cells, some of which then developed into organisms that, in turn, created a biosphere on the surface of the planet. When humans evolved, they brought an increased consciousness into existence. This consciousness then began to be linked by social structures, organizations, and communications. In 1925, Teilhard de Chardin coined the term *noosphere* to describe the global network of knowledge that he saw was beginning to encircle the planet. He believed that higher levels of "complexification" in the noosphere would lead to unification and a higher spiritual state for humanity. He would enjoy seeing how the noosphere, aided by a few photonic relay stations, permitted the laity of the church he served to find their collective voice.

—※—

I hope that Voice of the Faithful will grow with help from many sources, and in turn it will help the Catholic Church increase the good it can do. With the attention devoted to the sexual abuse scandal, it is easy to overlook all the good the church has done throughout the ages. The church has been a positive force in my own life in many ways, including the hierarchy's support of the work to prevent nuclear war. This was a dramatic example of the effectiveness of the church in promoting world peace. Catholic hospitals and clinics have provided health care to millions who otherwise would have suffered needlessly. Catholic social services work to diminish the poverty that exists alongside great wealth in contemporary society. Catholic schools and universities have educated hundreds of millions, who now comprise a knowledgeable laity ready to help their church in return. The church has also been a leader in its support of civil rights, and an advocate for immigrants as they become established in developed countries. In addition to these broader benefits to society, the church has supported ethical and moral studies. Scientific advances in genetics, reproductive medicine, and life-support capabilities now create complex situations in which individuals are required to confront difficult and novel choices. The teachings of the church and pastoral counseling now help individuals make these difficult decisions.

But perhaps the greatest temporal effect of the Catholic Church is achieved through the conversion of the hearts of its members to doing the best they can to follow the teachings of Christ. The strengths of Catholicism have created a church with a billion members worldwide that is growing rapidly in Africa and other parts of the developing world. In the United States the Catholic Church has 65 million members, making it by far the largest organized religion in the world's only superpower.

The primary source of the strength of Catholicism is the life and teachings of Jesus Christ. The church has preserved this precious deposit of faith in its words, if not always in its actions, for almost twenty centuries. Voice of the Faithful has arisen from the sex abuse scandal to prevent future scandals and help create a better church. This will occur only if the laity join together in great numbers and seize this opportunity to change their church.

CHAPTER 12

HOW WE CAN CHANGE THE CHURCH— TOGETHER

THE MOST IMPORTANT TRUTH I've learned since Voice of the Faithful formed in early 2002 is that the gravest threat to our church is not an abusive priest or arrogant bishop. I have learned from priests, theologians, historians, thousands of the faithful, and even some bishops that *the single greatest threat to the future of the Roman Catholic Church is continued complacency of the laity.*

The sexual abuse scandal, by giving rise to Voice of the Faithful and greater impetus to other activist organizations, creates an opportunity to solve the underlying problem of apathy among the Catholic laity. Millions are now actively re-examining their church and in so doing, ordinary Catholics are discovering their collective power.

As I contemplated the future of our group and the church, I was inspired by an idea from Jim Post. Jim suggested I go back to some of the founders of Voice of the Faithful and ask them about their highest hopes and dearest visions for the future. So I turned to men and women whom I have come to know as passionately devoted to making the Catholic Church a better place: Mary Scanlon, David Castaldi, Luise Dittrich, Svea and Scott Fraser, Mary Ann Keyes, Jim Post, Peggie Thorp, Steve Krueger, and Susan Troy. With their counsel I have identified some suggested activities for those who might like to become more actively involved in helping strengthen the church.

1. Join Voice of the Faithful.
2. Actively engage in dialogue about Catholicism.
3. Enhance the role of women in the church.
4. Support those who have been abused.
5. Reach out to lapsed Catholics.
6. Support priests of integrity.
7. Work to promote transparency and diminish the culture of clericalism and secrecy within the hierarchy.
8. Pursue the agenda of Cardinal Bernardin for reform of the church.
9. Pray—and keep the faith!

I realize that these suggestions are most likely to appeal to active Catholics who are already committed to changing the church. But I also hope some will appeal to angry, confused, and despondent Catholics who are thinking of leaving the church, to centrists who have not been active in debates about the church, and to conservatives, who have also been deeply affected by the abuse scandal. I hope they will also appeal to the millions of "lapsed Catholics" who remember many of the positive aspects of the church of their youth. If enough respond, it is possible to make our church better and stronger. Together, with the grace of God, our voices can make it so.

1. Join Voice of the Faithful.

Sister Joan Chittister, a well-known Catholic author, wrote in the *National Catholic Reporter* that she admired Voice because we were going after the "biggest issue of all: authority." Paul Lakeland, chairman of religious studies at Fairfield University, said that when he first heard about Voice of the Faithful he thought that our approach was "incredibly timid and deferential, but the longer it goes on, it becomes clear that what they really are doing is challenging the church on the authority issue, and therefore they are even more radical than they acknowledge being."

While there is no question that we are challenging the hierarchy on the issue of authority, I do not think of our group as radical because we are doing so based on principles advocated by Vatican II. The mission of Voice—"To provide a prayerful voice, attentive to the Spirit, through which the faithful can actively participate in the governance and guidance of the

Catholic Church"—provides a means to convert the principles of Vatican II into reality. Participating means having a certain amount of power—not power for its own sake, but the power to contribute so that thoughtful, intelligent decisions are made. That power will come from a strong Voice membership and many active affiliates working at the parish level. If you believe that it is important for the laity to have power—to engage in power sharing with the hierarchy—then the single most important step you can take is to join Voice of the Faithful. Why? Because there is strength in numbers.

Mary Ann Keyes, who helps organize Parish Voices throughout the country, observed, "Bringing our church to a better place in the twenty-first century will require the resolve and perseverance of the laity and the acceptance of lay involvement on all levels by the hierarchy. Voice's role is key to this end. There are inadequate structures in our church today for the layperson's voice to be heard. Our ability to awaken laity one person, one parish, one diocese at a time as to the importance of our voice in the reform of our church can best be accomplished through the framework of VOTF affiliates."

Joining Voice of the Faithful could not be easier. Simply go to our Web site (www.votf.org) and register, or mail your name and address to VOTF, P.O. Box 423, Newton Upper Falls, MA, 02464. Or call us at (617) 558-5252. Once registered, you are a member and you will receive regular e-mail updates on Voice activities, including our electronic newsletter, *In the Vineyard*, and our printed quarterly publication, *Voice*. Some of you will find upon joining that there is no affiliate in your parish. If that is the case, we warmly invite you to start a parish affiliate. Mary Ann Keyes at our national office can tell you precisely how to get a chapter up and running.

I would ask you, as a new member of Voice of the Faithful, to make a commitment to learning more about Catholicism through reading and reflection. (Many excellent readings are available on our Web site, and there are excellent books by a variety of authors mentioned throughout this book.) We also hope that you spread the word: Tell your family and friends that you've joined and explain why. Perhaps they, too, will want to consider joining.

2. Actively engage in dialogue about Catholicism.

Voice of the Faithful was born because a group of Catholics at St. John's parish needed to talk about the scandal. Our first session was nothing more than an opportunity to talk and listen and it proved enormously valuable. There was power inherent in the act of expressing how we felt and what we believed; of listening carefully to others who also loved the church; of absorbing the thoughts and passions articulated by others. Through dialogue, we have been enriched and enlightened.

Change in the Roman Catholic Church requires a common vision of the future. To achieve this we need to talk to one another as lay people, and to engage in a constructive—though perhaps sometimes contentious—dialogue with parish priests and other clergy, including nuns, as well as with the hierarchy.

The Catholic faithful historically have been mute as well as docile. Even people who are articulate and outspoken in the workplace and in community affairs tend toward silence in church activities. But that is changing.

"Catholics are talking to one another about their faith," observed Peggie Thorp. "Much of what is said is tough to hear; many Catholics are at loggerheads with each other." Yet this engagement, this dialogue on a variety of issues is itself a step forward. Peggie harkened back to our earliest listening sessions, which she and I led: "I cannot help but focus again and again on the act of listening, which is where VOTF started. I found myself recognizing just how large a family we really are—people with whom I disagree on many issues loved the same church I love, the same Christ. They felt the same hurt and horror I felt. . . . I recognized, as we all did, that Catholics had no precedent for this kind of dialogue—we were creating it, together. Today we are listening in new ways to our priests, and they to us. We are engaging in new ways with bishops and they with us. This is the future—*a refusal to be silenced.*"

Susan Troy envisioned a future where there is "the respectful exchange of understandings, hopes, beliefs, and doubts, between and among the church hierarchy, clergy, and faithful. If faith-filled, strenuous, and humble dialogue is the hallmark of the future, there will be a future for the church. Without this dialogue, this openness, this willingness to listen and learn from one another, the church will not survive. The institution might survive, but only as an anemic shadow of what might have been."

Luise Dittrich said simply that in an improved church, "inquiry and discussion are welcomed, not suppressed."

Part of engaging in dialogue means participating in some of the vibrant programs being run at various Catholic universities. The Boston College program *The Church in the 21st Century* is an ideal example. It affords Catholics and others a chance to listen to a wide range of intellectuals and to engage in a colloquy about the great issues of our faith—and much of the material is available on the Boston College Web site (www.bc.edu).

3. Enhance the role of women in the church.

Increasing the role of women in the guidance and governance of the church would have profound implications. Imagine this scene: Cardinal Law is gathered in the elegant residence at the Boston chancery with several of his key advisers. All are dressed in black. All are men. In this hushed environment where major decisions are made, there is *never* a woman present. But on this day, as the Cardinal has his key people around him, the chancery door suddenly opens and in walks Svea Fraser or Mary Scanlon or Susan Troy or any one of countless active Catholic women. The meeting commences and one of the staff members reports that a fellow priest has sexually abused children in a particular parish. What to do about it?

One of Cardinal Law's closest advisers suggests transferring the priest to another parish. Absolute secrecy will be maintained—no one must know what has happened. Around the table, heads nod in agreement. At this point, Svea or Mary or Susan would speak up. They would explain to these unmarried men that the health and safety of children must always come first—before all else. This is the enormous value of the perspective and experience of a woman.

As Luise Dittrich said in response to the earliest news of the sex abuse scandal: "This is what happens when you don't have women involved, when you don't have married people involved. If women were involved, this could never possibly have happened."

"There is a powerful temptation to allow the status quo because it is comfortable and familiar, and because we really do appreciate traditions of the past and want to pass those on to succeeding generations," said Mary Scanlon. "The tension between maintaining the past and claiming one's legitimate place in the culture of a society is familiar to women, so it may be that the renewal in the church will be best understood by and enacted by women, especially since it is women who traditionally educate and indoctrinate the next generation. The challenge will be in knowing when to accept and when to resist the established authority. . . . I think that if the patriarchy in power at present is able to exclude other constituencies, it will have a devastating effect on the church, making it increasingly less relevant to the lived experience of Catholics."

Susan Troy is an example of a woman who has contributed much to the church. The knowledge she obtained during study for her master's of divinity degree has helped her to contribute mightily to St. John's parish. The liturgy she planned with Sister Evelyn Ronan and others stands today as a masterpiece of the time. And yet this same woman was ignored by bishops at their Washington conference.

Susan has a strong grasp of the church's traditions. "Even before bishops and uniform rites, there were lives lived in love and service because of an individual's experience of Christ, his life and message, and the conversion of their hearts. How did the peoples of the Mediterranean identify Christians in their midst? They were the ones inviting all to the table, caring for the poorest in the cities and in the country, with women in leadership roles, with outcasts welcomed and cared for as brothers and sisters. They were the counterculturists of their day. This is the future of the church. If we become known for the quality of our lives, the robustness of individual faith made present in the home, in the workplace, in the world . . . if they know we are Christians and Catholics by our actions and by our communion and by our love for each other, then we will know that we are truly a church, and that we are indeed an instrument of God's love and God's peace."

Shirley and Dick Fennel have been among the strongest supporters of Voice. At a meeting to discuss future priorities, Dick noted that our group would have difficulty recruiting new members as the sexual abuse scandal diminished. "People will want to see VOTF addressing an important new issue," he argued. The issue, he said, should be the role of women in the church. "Women are Catholicism's greatest supporters, yet they are treated with little respect. VOTF should take on this issue."

Jim Post offered his perspective. "There are two great fault lines in our church today. I am convinced that irreparable damage is being done by the institutional refusal to understand and address human sexuality on the one hand, and the refusal to embrace the full contribution of women to the life of the church on the other. . . . I think that theologians and bishops will eventually discern that the patterns of history are not eternal mandates. It is beyond my ability to know how this will transpire, and I cannot say when or where it will happen, but I believe this will be revealed to people of good will in due course.

"In this life, men and women are blessed with equal intelligence, equal capacity to reason, equal capacity to pray, and equal capacity to love. We are taught that the souls of men and women will be indistinguishable in heaven. If gender does not determine talent and ability in this life, or status in the next, why does it serve as the fulcrum on which full participation in the life of the church turns?"

I share Jim's view. I believe the lack of a voice for women is one of the factors limiting the appeal of Catholicism to the next generation. I wish it were different, and I believe that it can be. The Vatican has declared that the issue of women's ordination cannot be discussed. But there are countless other ways to enhance the role of women at the parish level and beyond.

One particular reform that I believe would have an immediate and enormously positive effect worldwide: Permit women to serve as deacons. With the increasingly acute shortage of priests, deacons are playing an ever-greater role in church life. Deacons may not absolve sins or consecrate the Eucharist, but they are empowered to baptize and preach as well as preside at marriages and funerals. Deacons perform works of charity with the poor and sick, and they often are involved in teaching religious education and preparing for sacraments.

The diaconate was created in the early church to recruit people who would help with a variety of tasks. But as Catholicism and the number of priests grew through the years, the need for deacons was reduced. The diaconate hibernated, in effect, for about one thousand years, until it was restored in 1968.

Today, only men are permitted to become deacons—even married men. Interestingly, when a married man is in training to become a deacon, his wife is required to go through the training with him. But though she has been part of training, she is barred from serving her church as a deacon.

"I believe many would welcome women in the diaconate," said Svea, "especially in a church that welcomed the gifts of all people of God."

I hope that Voice, through its elected representatives, will debate and take a stand on this issue. If it recommends that women be permitted to serve as deacons, and the hierarchy agrees with that proposal, what a positive signal about Catholicism would be sent throughout the world.

4. Support those who have been abused.

"For the rest of their lives, the survivors are our trust," observed Peggie Thorp. "They taught us what listening meant and how to do it. . . . Like prophets before them, the survivors weren't always and everywhere recognized. It took their courage to empower our voices, but first we had to *hear* them. For a long time we didn't know how to talk with survivors—in the beginning we called them victims. The survivors chose their own label and we have honored it ever since. I remember a very early meeting of about two hundred people in the basement of St. John the Evangelist Church in Wellesley. We were close to consensus on our three goals, the first of which was to support survivors. A woman sitting up front raised her hand, stood, and said, 'What do you mean by support?' There was a scramble of responses, but the outcome was an understanding that it would not be the rest of us defining that term—it would be the survivors. What we wanted to give would not always be what they needed to get. To this day, it seems to me that what survivors continue to ask is that we stand with them—literally. Leave what we're doing and stand with them—in civil protest, in prayer, in silence, in solidarity."

Susan Troy and Sister Evelyn Ronan and others at Voice of the Faithful showed us the transcendent beauty of a healing mass—a liturgy focused on survivors and the need for healing and reconciliation. That evening at St. John's for me—and I know for many others as well—was profound. The text of that liturgy is on the Voice Web site, and we hope Catholics elsewhere might host a liturgy for survivors and their loved ones as a tangible expression of their concern.

It is important for Catholics to make an effort to reach out to survivors and tell them of our respect and admiration for their ability to survive. It is so helpful to support them and pray for them, to stand by them at vigils and prayer meetings, to contribute financially to survivor groups such as the Survivors' Network of those Abused by Priests (www.snapnetwork.org) or the LinkUp (www.thelinkup.org).

5. Reach out to lapsed Catholics.

No one is sure of the precise number, but we do know that Catholics have left the church in droves. They have left over church policies on issues such as birth control, divorce, and abortion. They have left because of the church's attitude toward women and gays. They have left because they grew up attending a rigid Catholic school and couldn't wait to escape. They have left because of the termination of the Latin mass and the loss of the mystical power of the liturgy. They have left because there has been so little dialogue, so little effort on the part of the hierarchy to listen to what is on the minds of lay people. They left because they had serious concerns about the religion and no effective way to address those concerns.

Most of those who left did so *before* the priest sex abuse scandals. Tens of millions in the United States alone describe themselves as "lapsed" Catholics. Many of these individuals value their Catholic heritage and sense an absence in their lives that the church once filled. They will not, however, consider rejoining the church as it was, let alone as it has been revealed to be by the sexual abuse cover-up. On hearing the details of the scandal, a friend of mine who considered herself a lapsed Catholic asked if there was a category even farther removed from the church than "lapsed." That might be the group described by Bill Keller of the *New York Times* as "collapsed."

In late 2003, on the occasion of the twenty-fifth anniversary of Pope John Paul II becoming the bishop of Rome, both the *New York Times* and the *Wall Street Journal* devoted significant time and space to special reports on the broad crisis of Catholicism. Reporter Frank Bruni of the *Times*, focusing on Europe, observed, "Europe already seems more and more like a series of tourist-trod monuments to Christianity's past. Hardly a month goes by when the pope does not publicly bemoan that fact, beseeching Europeans to rediscover the faith."

Journal reporters John Carreyrou, Matt Murray, James Hookway, and Jose deCordoba wrote that in Europe today "the Catholic faith is a shadow of its former self in countries such as Italy, Spain, France and Ireland. Though a majority of their citizens still describe themselves as Catholic, attendance at Mass has declined, in some countries sharply, as has the number of priests. The Continent's ancient churches and cathedrals fill up with tourists, not parishioners."

David Castaldi observed that the sexual abuse crisis "eroded the esteem in which many lay Catholics hold some or all of the hierarchy. When any organization . . . has many members reluctant to follow its leaders, it is in distress." David pointed to a tangible sign of the distress—a survey indicating that in Boston only about 15 percent of Catholics attended mass on an average Sunday.

"Our Church could become like the Church in many parts of Western Europe where Sunday liturgy is celebrated in nearly vacant churches," David said. "I hope and pray for a renewed Church that can attract more Catholics to worship God. Such renewal requires many changes in the human institutional life of the Church. Our bishops need to visit and dialogue with parish worship communities. Our parishes and our diocesan operations must have meaningful and broadly representative cooperation with the laity in the administration of Church affairs. The laity needs to understand and accept the teaching authority of the Church and the roles of bishops rooted in our scripture and tradition as our primary leaders and teachers."

In 2003, Tina MacVeigh, a young Catholic professional in her early thirties, attended a Voice of the Faithful meeting I led at St. Francis de Sales Church in Cincinnati. I asked if she could explain the absence of young people at the event. She later wrote that young people were not well represented in Voice because most had already left the church. As for the reason, she added, "As a young person I have a voice in my government; as an employee I have a personal voice in my employment; and as a stockholder I have a voice in the company I work for. Where is my voice in the church?"

Since absence of a voice is the problem Voice is designed to correct, I was not surprised by Tina's closing words. "I came to the [Voice] session without much expectation and I left inspired. I see hope."

I believe that if we can strengthen that voice and if we can succeed in continuing the ongoing dialogue which has already begun, we will win back countless lapsed Catholics who will see that the institution is at least willing to give voice to the laity; that it is at least willing to discuss some issues which are so important to so many.

We need a determined effort within the church—and here Voice could play an effective missionary role—to go out and actively work to persuade lapsed Catholics to return to the faith and give it another chance. To be effective, observed Jim Post, the church must be "inclusive and welcoming to all people. Too many of us are watching our children and grandchildren—the next generations—being driven away by divisive policies and practices of current leaders. Jesus welcomed all women and men to His flock. Repeatedly, however, we see the Vatican and American bishops pursuing policies that separate and divide people, rather than bringing us together."

I believe that there is a spiritual hunger out there. The words of Ladislaus Orsy, S. J., echo in my mind: "You cannot reject the body without losing the soul sooner or later." It is a chilling notion—that those who fall away from the religion may very well eventually lose their faith.

Invite a lapsed Catholic to join you in attending a Voice of the Faithful meeting and show her that the powerlessness that may have led her to leave the church is changing; show her that there is a legitimate outlet to assert the lay voice and to discuss topics that heretofore have been silently accepted.

Many lapsed Catholics are spiritually poorer for having fallen away; we are all poorer for having lost them; and our institution is immeasurably weaker without them. We have to make sure that we create a church where the laity have enough of a say so that lapsed Catholics will want to return.

6. Support priests of integrity.

Simple signs of support can mean a great deal to a priest. If you are inspired by the priest or priests in your parish, a word after mass or a letter about how he has helped you can have great effect. As can a letter to the bishop commending him. Inviting your parish priest into your home for dinner with your family or with others from your parish is a wonderful gesture. The life of a parish priest is difficult and enormously challenging, and getting more so each day as the numbers of priests declines. According to *America Magazine*, during the past twenty years in major Protestant religions, ordinations have increased 21 to 35 percent. During the same period Catholic ordinations have declined 21 percent. A decade ago, there was one priest for every eight hundred Catholics. Now there is one priest for every 1,428 people. In light of these sobering statistics, it is especially important that priests know they are recognized and supported.

Those who wish to join Voice might ask their priest if he is familiar with Voice of the Faithful. If he is and finds value in our organization, perhaps he might bring it to the attention of parishioners. Voice has grown most effectively in parishes where the pastor is supportive. Likewise, since the earliest days of our group, when Sister Evelyn Ronan played such an important role, religious women have provided great strength to Voice. And their continued support of Voice is essential.

7. Work to promote transparency and diminish the culture of clericalism and secrecy within the hierarchy.

The corporate scandals in recent years offer a useful lesson to the Catholic Church. Companies with secretive cultures that permitted deception and cover-up have met with disastrous fates. On the other hand, firms that are transparent and open, that welcome the views of their shareholders, that engage in an ongoing dialogue with their shareholders—these are the companies that thrive in the modern world.

Is there any question that the church's culture of secrecy has enabled deception and corruption to occur? It is worth recalling the words of Father Tom Doyle, the winner of the Priest of Integrity Award at our convention. "The primary symptom of [clericalism] is the delusion that the clergy are somehow above the laity, deserving of unquestioned privilege and stature, the keepers of our salvation and the guarantors of our favor with the Lord. *The deadliest symptom however is the unbridled addiction to power.* . . . This widespread and deeply ingrained abuse of power by the hierarchical leadership of our Church has been sustained and even encouraged by the myth that what is good for that tiny minority, the clergy, is identified with what is good for the Church."

Anthony Massimini, a Voice leader in Philadelphia and former priest, contends, "The clerical culture has no basis in church teaching. It is an historic accretion that has been built up over the centuries by certain events, such as the church's inheritance of ancient male-dominant, patriarchal society structures."

Scott and Svea Fraser identified two keys for a successful future church—one leading to the other: "the elimination of the culture of clericalism that dominates the church today and the creation (and acceptance by the hierarchy) of robust institutional mechanisms that enable the laity to have a real voice in the governance and guidance of the temporal affairs of the church. Progress in these two areas will require substantial changes in the attitudes, values, norms, and behavior of the laity, the clergy, and the hierarchy. This will take time. In addition to prayer, it will require education, reflection, dialogue, experimentation, and mutual respect for our respective talents."

8. Pursue the agenda of Cardinal Bernardin for reform of the church.

Most of the topics discussed above are contained in a comprehensive list of crucial discussion points for Catholics compiled by Cardinal Joseph L. Bernardin. I had the great honor of working with this leader of the hierarchy during the movement to prevent nuclear war. He reminded me of Father Theodore Hesburgh, the superb leader of Notre Dame when I was an undergraduate.

Cardinal Bernardin was a man of humble beginnings, the son of immigrant parents who rose to become one of the most influential and beloved Catholic bishops in the world. He was the principal author of *Challenge of Peace*, the U.S. bishops' pastoral letter on nuclear war, published in 1983. He was a man who recognized the importance of Catholics engaging in active dialogue and he welcomed and encouraged it. In fact, he recognized the divisive nature of conflict between Catholic liberals and conservatives, and he founded the Common Ground Initiative so that Catholics of differing views could engage in open, healthy dialogue.

As explained by Peter Steinfels in *A People Adrift*, Cardinal Bernardin created a list of the critical issues facing the church and framed them in a manner that he hoped would be acceptable to all. The Bernardin agenda is an excellent starting point for topics that the laity, with democratically selected representatives, should consider discussing.

- The changing roles of women
- The organization and effectiveness of religious education
- The eucharistic liturgy as most Catholics experience it
- The meaning of human sexuality, and the gap between church teachings and the convictions of many faithful in this and several other areas of morality
- The image and morale of priests, and the declining ratios of priests and vowed religious people to people in the pews
- The succession of lay people to positions of leadership formerly held by priests and sisters, and the provision of an adequate formation for ministers, both ordained and lay
- The ways in which the church is present in political life, its responsibility to the poor and defenseless, and its support for lay people in their family lives and daily callings
- The capacity of the church to embrace African-American, Latino, and Asian populations, their cultural heritages, and their social concerns
- The survival of Catholic school systems, colleges and universities, health care facilities and social services, and the articulation of a distinct and appropriate religious identity and mission for these institutions

- The dwindling financial support from parishioners
- The manner of decision making and consultation in church governance
- The responsibility of theology to authoritative church teachings
- The place of collegiality and subsidiarity in relations between Rome and the American episcopacy

Unfortunately, as Cardinal Bernardin was dying in 1996, his agenda was attacked by autocratic cardinals and bishops opposed to his efforts at dialogue with the laity. The attackers preferred to consider church teaching on these issues as unchangeable. The leader of this attack was Cardinal Bernard Law, who at the same time was covering up crimes against children. My hope is that Voice will now pursue the critical issues of the Bernardin agenda using its powerful democratic processes.

Voice is also suited to assist with changes in the church as framed by Father Thomas Reese, S. J., the editor of the prestigious Jesuit publication *America* as quoted in David Gibson's book *The Coming Catholic Church*. Father Reese calls for three levels of reform: of governance, of policies, and of attitude. Gibson reviews these three levels and notes that one will flow from the other in the order in which they are mentioned. Clearly Voice members intend to participate in the governance of the church, and much of the reform of governance that is needed is an increase in participation by the laity, as advocated by Vatican II. With regard to policies, members of Voice intend to be involved in the guidance of the church; it has created a democratic structure to permit the laity to form and express their views on many policies of the Church. Finally, Voice has attempted to improve the attitudes among those who have conflicting views of the best course for Catholicism. Voice is engaged in respectful dialogue with bishops, even those that oppose the group, and we welcome views from Catholics of all persuasions.

While the issues identified by Cardinal Bernardin affect the worldwide church, it appears that the American Catholic Church can play a special role in their resolution. Although we have encouraged the growth of Voice in Ireland, Germany, Australia, New Zealand, and elsewhere, it has not spread nearly as rapidly internationally as in the United States where Catholicism has distinct features favoring change. The special gifts that the American Catholic Church offers to the universal church have been described by Father Roger Haight, a Jesuit theologian at the Weston Jesuit School of Theology in Massachusetts. The first is the concept of religious freedom, as articulated by John Courtney Murray, and already incorporated into church teaching. The other three are available, but not yet fully utilized. They are: experience with the role of women in the church, the positive evaluation of other religions, and the increased role of the laity—a role that has now become more explicit with the emergence of Voice.

9. Pray—and keep the faith!

It is easy to become discouraged and conclude that the task of changing a two-thousand-year-old institution of one billion members is not possible. But when the Holy Spirit is playing a role, massive change is possible. Some positive changes have recently occurred. The mere existence of Voice of the Faithful as a channel for an independent lay voice is important. It gives me a sense of optimism about the future of the church because I know there are millions of Catholics of goodwill who love their faith and want their church to change for the better.

Many Catholics wonder if they can ever again trust their religion. Father Orsy addressed the issue of the role of the crisis and the future of Catholicism in a speech at Boston College. "Was the crisis allowed by God to help the church come to the end of an era?" he asked a gathering of faculty and students. "To open the door to new developments?" He said he believed that in the church, when there is a "great crisis, a great gift is coming."

The good news is that change is already apparent. "For the next generation, maybe two, Catholics will continue to do what VOTF started in January 2002—move toward a sea change in the way laity relate to the church, and vice versa," said Peggie Thorp. "This is the good news of our moment. Already I don't recognize the church I attended and supported all of my life, and already I know this new place of uncertainty, risk, challenge, discovery, and enormous effort is a better place."

David Castaldi keeps the faith because he believes in the guidance of the Holy Spirit. "I am convinced that God wants lay people to play a meaningful and significant role in helping the ordained leaders of our church in the future, and if I am correct, then the Holy Spirit will guide the church in that direction. There is an old saying [From Saint Ignatius Loyola, founder of the Jesuits]: *Pray as if everything depends on God, and work as if everything depends on you.* If God wants meaningful lay involvement in all aspects of our church, and if we work toward that objective and do it out of faith and love for our church, eventually recalcitrant bishops will see the light. This is what God expects of his church."

—∞—

When we began Voice of the Faithful in February of 2002, we did not anticipate such a momentous journey, nor did we expect to be attacked by leaders of our church for our efforts to *help* the church. Many of us involved in Voice genuinely believed that the hierarchy would accept our offer of a partnership for the good of the church.

But instead of welcoming us, the Boston hierarchy threw down the gauntlet. Did we have any choice but to pick it up? Was there any other course but to accept the challenge? Anything we could do other than fight back?

As I look back on the journey of Voice, there are many inspiring people and moments—the courageous survivors who made our movement possible; Father Tom Powers encouraging our dialogue; our early meetings of just a handful of people; the women in red at the cardinal's convocation; the power of our healing mass for survivors; the army of volunteers at our landmark convention; courageous members of the Boston Priest's Forum; the good bishops who do not oppose us; the theologians who spoke out in support of us; the spirit of Vatican II.

I believe these gifts were given by the Spirit, in a time of darkness, to start a movement to make the Catholic Church stronger and better than it has ever been. If this promising beginning of Voice of the Faithful is now strengthened by the millions of Catholics who also seek to keep the faith, together we will surely change the church.

ACKNOWLEDGMENTS

Much of the material in this book is based on Dr. James Muller's personal observation of events. The story has been enriched by interviews conducted by Charles Kenney with key members of Voice of the Faithful. For their time, recollections, and invaluable insights, we are particularly indebted to Paul Baier, Luise Cahill Dittrich, David Castaldi, Svea and Scott Fraser, Steve Krueger, Jim Post, Mary Scanlon, Peggie Thorp, and Susan Troy.

We are grateful to our wives, Kathleen and Anne, for their counsel throughout the process of writing this book.

For sharing their ideas, thoughts, and recollections, we are grateful to Arthur Austin; Father Robert Bullock; Tanya Chermak; Ernie Corrigan; Tim and Julie Dempsey; Father Tom Doyle; Mike Emerton; Cathy and Bill Fallon; Andrea Johnson; Mary Ann Keyes; Terry McKiernan; Ladislaus Orsy, S. J.; Father Gerald Osterman; Jeannette Post, M. D.; and Phil Saviano.

We owe an enormous debt to the *Boston Globe*, whose coverage of the sex abuse scandal beginning in January 2002 earned the paper the Pulitzer Prize for public service in 2003 and was invaluable to the writing of this book. We are indebted to the entire *Globe* team responsible for the coverage, including editor

Martin Baron, deputy managing editor Benjamin Bradlee Jr., Spotlight editor Walter V. Robinson, and reporters Matt Carroll, Kevin Cullen, Thomas Farragher, Stephen A. Kurkjian, Sacha Pfeiffer, and Michael Rezendes, and Michael Paulson played a particularly important role with his chronicling of the rapid evolution of Voice. We relied upon many *Globe* articles for details and quotations from participants in the story, particularly involving Cardinal Law and other members of the hierarchy. Pam Belluck of the *New York Times* also provided insightful reporting that was useful in the writing of this book.

Arthur Austin kindly allowed us to present the text of the dramatic speech he delivered at our convention (chapter 8); the speech is copyrighted and used with his permission. Father Tom Doyle also granted us permission to quote from his fine speech.

We are also grateful to Kathi Aldridge, Barbara Blaine, David Clohessy, Jack Connors, Ann Barrett Doyle, Father William Kremmell, James Mahoney, Anthony Massimini, Terry Meehan, Paul F. Muller, M. D., Maura O'Brien, Tommy and Jackie O'Neill, Father John Philbin, Steve Pope, Father Thomas Powers, John and Mary Riley, Sister Evelyn Ronan, Margaret Roylance, Pat Serrano, Tom Smith, and Tom White.

Luise Cahill Dittrich, in addition to her role with Voice, provided research help for the book. Dr. Robert Kloner reviewed an early draft. Father Richard McBrien and Roger Haight, S. J., reviewed portions of the manuscript for accuracy.

We are grateful to Stephanie Tade of Rodale, who saw the potential importance of this book, and to Chris Potash of Rodale, whose fine editorial sense improved the manuscript.

DATE DUE

#47-0108 Peel Off Pressure Sensitive